Building Bridges

Building Bridges

by

Catherine Hollingworth

O.B.E., F.R.A.M., F.C.S.T., F.E.I.S.

The Pentland Press Limited
Edinburgh · Cambridge · Durham

First published in 1993 by
The Pentland Press Ltd.
1 Hutton Close
South Church
Bishop Auckland
Durham

ISBN 1 85821 107 7

Typeset by Elite Typesetting Techniques, Southampton.
Printed and bound by Antony Rowe Ltd., Chippenham.

This book is dedicated to my cousin, Dr. George Manson O.B.E., lately G.P. in Peterhead. His wide interest in, and care for, other people are characteristics of a good doctor. Over the years, 'Mutt' has consistently shown great concern and courtesy to me, for which I am most appreciative.

Contents

Contents

List of Illustrations

Acknowledgements

The first person I wish to thank is Evie Melvin. To her I entrusted all the tapes which I had made while I was confined to bed. I handed them to her unmarked and in a state of complete disorganisation; I had simply recorded all I could remember of times past up to the present just as it came to me. The fact that all this has been transformed into an ordered narrative is due first and foremost to Evie's devoted work and care. To have produced a manuscript from such material seems nothing short of miraculous.

I am also indebted to Sylvia Robinson, an old friend who, many years ago, was on the staff of the Speech and Drama Department, and who also worked in the Children's Theatre, the Mobile Theatre and the Longacre Players. Besides all this, she co-operated generously, happily and unstintingly in every possible way in the work of the Department. Since those days twenty-five years have passed, thirteen of them spent in Dundee and twelve in Aberdeen, yet I still remember Sylvia's contribution to the Department with the utmost pleasure and happiness. It was she, therefore, who, knowing the background as she did, took the material to the next stage, reducing the script to some kind of order, a task which, in my blindness, I would otherwise have found impossible. Without having Sylvia to read it to me I would have been quite helpless.

A further invaluable aid has been the advice of Alan Cowie, now Assistant News Editor with Grampian Television. I remember him as a little boy in particularly short shorts. Together with his Grammar School cronies Malcolm Rennie and Kenny Christie, he acted in the Children's Theatre, and a more delightful trio of little horrors could not be imagined!

Finally I wish to acknowledge my indebtedness to Edwin Grieve, my solicitor, who, in the interest he has shown in my story and in researching the possibilities of publication, has played a vital part in enabling the book to materialise.

These therefore are the friends who have helped me with its actual production, and I thank them all. However I must also thank all those others, from all walks of life, who helped me in my work in Aberdeen right from the time when I first arrived there, not quite realising at that stage what I was trying to do. I found their kindness a major source of encouragement and though at the time it may have seemed little to them, to me it was deeply important. I cannot therefore lose the present opportunity of expressing to all these too my deep and sincere thanks.

Foreword

Shortly after I arrived in Aberdeen in January 1946, I met a remarkable lady – Catherine Hollingworth. Just how remarkable she was I learned gradually in the years that followed and my admiration for her grew.

In an inspired decision the City of Aberdeen Education Committee had appointed this pioneer to a new post – ill-defined at the time – to improve the standard of the spoken word. I suspect that Catherine was appointed on the basis of her previous training and interests, coupled with her buoyant personality and enthusiasm for the importance of speech – 'man's greatest gift'.

This appointment was the start of a new adventure for Catherine and for the Committee and, in time, for countless boys and girls, teachers and parents and many adults who asked for help and were never refused.

It is only in retrospect that we can try to assess the effects on our future lives and careers of family and friends, interests, events and circumstances of our childhood and youth.

Catherine's self-analysis of her background culminated in her interest in education, speech and drama and finally speech therapy. She could not have chosen a better apprenticeship for her future career if she had been endowed with the gift of foresight. Perhaps she was!

Her personal qualities, which served her well, were vision, drive, enthusiasm and imagination along with a love of children, an appreciation of standards of discipline and courtesy, a disregard for self – she works all hours – and all laced with a sense of humour. These shine through in the pages of her story.

And what a story it is! Starting on her own, she developed her work until she became official superintendent of speech and speech therapy – a

unique appointment in the country and possibly one that will never
be repeated. But then there was and is only one Catherine Hollingworth.

I recall many of the significant incidents along the way. Back in the late
40s there were the attempts to obtain suitable accommodation for the
children's activities in a period when space was at a premium. Despite the
difficulties she kept going, succeeding and seeing her work expand. In
time the Committee managed to improve the provision of accommodation
and Catherine's brilliant innovation and development of a Children's
Theatre became a reality – of which she had every reason to be proud. The
Aberdeen Children's Theatre was different in a variety of ways from
others of its kind and exemplified Catherine's individual approach as to
what she considered best in provision of this kind. How right she proved
to be.

As Head of Department she had to submit an Annual Report to the
Education Committee. This was circulated to members and Catherine was
present when it was discussed. I know how she agonised over the writing
of these Reports, but how important they were! The Committee learned of
progress and discussed future developments. What a pride the members
took in her work and what she and her colleagues had achieved and how
sympathetic they were to how she wanted the Department to develop! The
proof of that is seen in the healthy state of her expanded Department when
she retired in 1968.

Catherine tells of the many important methods by which she furthered
her work – festivals of different kinds, puppetry, work in schools with
teachers – many of whom were only too keen to assist with the Children's
Theatre and other out-of-school ventures.

It is impossible to know with any degree of accuracy what Catherine
Hollingworth's contribution meant to so many in Aberdeen and to the
reputation of education in the city and far beyond. This I can say as
Director: I was immensely proud of her outstanding services over so many
years. No other Education Area had a Catherine Hollingworth.

I am honoured and delighted to have been asked to contribute this
foreword to the autobiography of one who was undoubtedly pre-eminent
in her field of educational endeavour. She gave so much pleasure to so
many – not least to myself in our many discussions over the years and on
many occasions when I saw the fruits of her labours in her various
activities. Thank you, Catherine.

Finally I share the delight of many that she has agreed to tell her story.
More importantly, that she dictated it, for it is the article of her faith that
'the spoken word' is supreme.

Catherine Hollingworth has indeed built her own bridges well!

> J.R. Clark CBE. MA, BSc, MEd, FEIS,
> Director of Education,
> City of Aberdeen, 1955–1975

Introduction

Many of those who have read Alan Nicol's book, 'Tilting at Windmills' have telephoned or spoken to me personally to say how much they enjoyed it. All, however, suggested that I should write a far fuller account of my life. My reaction to this persistent message has come to be: 'Well, I had better get on with it. After all, I am in my ninetieth year and have not all that much time left!' The question has been where to begin.

Yesterday the answer came – at least in part. A District Nurse visited me to remove some wax from my ear. She was wearing what to me seemed a novel kind of uniform consisting of blue trousers and a white jumper. Attractive though it was, it was so unfamiliar to me that until she explained the situation I took her for a physiotherapist. Before starting work on my ear, we had a few minutes' conversation. 'As you know,' I said, 'I have lost my sight, I have lost my hearing, and though I haven't lost a leg, it doesn't work and I'm very lame.' 'Well,' she replied, 'you haven't lost your sense of humour, have you?' Though at first I could not understand what had prompted this remark, it did raise one question in my mind: 'Is it a trait that I have inherited?' That led on to the further question, 'What other qualities have I inherited, and from whom?' I then embarked on an attempt to trace some of the particular characteristics that have manifested themselves throughout the eighty-nine years of my life, especially those which seemed to appear in the lives of my ancestors before me. My conclusions are set forth in the pages which follow.

This approach has greatly influenced the record of my life as it emerged, with all its twists and turns, most of them quite unpremeditated. As I look back, I realise how little of my life has been planned, how large a part circumstances have played in mapping its course. Again and again I have reacted to some fresh experience by saying: 'I want to know a bit more about this.' In the case of speech therapy it was: 'I will have to go and find out what speech therapy is'; in the case of the puppets, 'I must go and see how they work'. It was never the outcome of clearcut or deliberate planning.

6th August, 1992

PART I. HAPPY DISCOVERIES

'I shall be telling with a sigh
Somewhere ages and ages hence;
Two roads diverged in a wood and I –
I took the one less travelled by,
And that has made all the difference.'

From 'The Road Not Taken' by Robert Frost

Chapter One

Family Background

My story begins in October, 1732, when a certain George Inglis married Christian Matthewson. These were destined to become my great, great, great, great-grandparents. Their son, David Inglis, was born two years later in 1734 and eventually married one Christian Urquhart. Though little is known of these two generations of my family, with the following one the story becomes fuller and clearer. David Inglis, their son and my great, great-grandfather, was born in 1771 in the parish of Dairsie in Fife. He subsequently became the first minister of the little church at Loch Lee in what has since become the parish of Glen Esk in the County of Angus.

Originally a teacher, he fell in love with a certain Catherine Collier, the daughter of the factor of an outstandingly large estate, and wanted to marry her. As a mere teacher, however, he was not considered good enough for her, and in order to achieve his ambition, became a minister. He must have wanted her very deeply.

For over thirty years he and his wife lived in the manse at Loch Lee, which was situated in a beautiful glen. Every year I used to spend a month of my summer holidays at Glen Esk, first as a little girl and then as an adolescent. My first visit, when I was about eleven, turned out to be momentous. In company with three other girls, Maggie Scott, Nan Scot and a third, whose name I cannot now remember, I arranged with the local joiner to hire a caravan and horse in which he drove us up from Brechin. About a month later he returned to take us home. That was my first visit to the Glen, and I remember being struck, even then, by its majesty. At the time, however, I had no knowledge of this ancestry of mine.

Let us return to my great, great-grandfather. The story goes that one day a man came riding over the Grampians from the Deeside road and drew rein as he arrived at the stables beside the manse, where he saw a man

My great grandfather, David Inglis.

working. 'Here, my man,' said the horseman, 'Will you stable my horse? I am going in to the hotel for a bite to eat.' The supposed stableman was, of course, none other than my great, great-grandfather while the 'hotel' was the manse. Under the circumstances he might reasonably have replied: 'I'm sorry, I am not the stable boy, I am the minister here, but I will see that your horse is fed and watered,' or even: 'This is a manse, not an hotel, but my wife will give you something to eat.' Instead, he simply left it at that and did as he was bid. Only when he himself returned to the manse, did he introduce himself to the stranger, who was meanwhile enjoying a good meal supplied by Mrs. Inglis. Obviously this ancestor of mine had a sense of humour, and I should like to think that that is an attribute which I have inherited.

David Inglis had a family of six. When they were old enough, two of his sons set out on foot to enrol as students at the University of Aberdeen. Carrying sacks of meal on their backs, they crossed the drove road that lay in the shelter of Mount Keane, and from this reached the Deeside Road leading to their destination. The younger of the two was to become a minister, the elder decided to be a doctor. He was my great-grandfather, so let us concentrate on him.

For four years, from 1817 to 1821, he studied medicine at Aberdeen. The course, however, is said to have been badly organised and most of those who aimed at becoming doctors went to Glasgow or Edinburgh. In David's case he left the University at the end of the four years without graduating and returned to the place where, I believe, his heart must have been – Glen Esk.

He took the farm of the Baillies above Tarfside, and subsequently married a certain Margaret Clark, who came from Montrose. She was the daughter of a Captain Clark who, as far as I can remember, was in charge of the militia at Montrose until the time of Waterloo, when it was disbanded. A particularly beautiful silver bowl has survived from this period, which was left in such a way as to go down the female line of the family. It bears the inscription: 'To Captain Clark, from the Officers of the Militia'. An exquisite piece of silver, it eventually came to my mother. As my mother did not want it, my grandmother left it to her youngest daughter, who in turn left it to her eldest daughter. I have often wondered about the admissibility of this arrangement and whether my great-aunt was legally entitled to make a gift of the bowl. I have even tried to persuade my cousin to let the Scottish National Museum have so historic a piece of silverware as it unquestionably is. So far I have failed to achieve this, but I feel strongly that it should be made available to a wider public to enjoy.

David Inglis of The Bailies.

To return to David and his wife from Montrose. They lived at the Bailies and eventually produced nine children there, four boys and five girls, of whom the second youngest was my grandmother, Catherine Jane Clark Burnett. She was born in 1852. David had some interesting traits. A hard worker and original thinker, he introduced on his farm a whole range of techniques of husbandry which were far ahead of his time. Many of his plans for the cultivation of his land were, in fact, highly original. He enlarged his farm by taking in some of the surrounding ones. Above all, he sought the permission of the laird to build a little school. At the time, it seems, an Episcopal church and Episcopal school were already in existence, but as a Church of Scotland man, my grandfather had no wish for a school run on Episcopalian lines. It had to be a Church of Scotland school. The laird refused, but when David asked permission to build a sheepcote, he agreed. As soon as it was built, David employed a teacher to teach the children who gathered from all the surrounding farms and crofts as well as his own sons and daughters. Thus in spite of all obstacles, a little school was set up, which also served as a church on Sundays, especially after the Disruption. For at this juncture David and his brother Robert opted for the Free Church. I believe that the foundations of that school are still visible to this day from the drove road as it runs just beyond Tarfside.

Here, then, is an ancestor who had the courage of his convictions and who was prepared to work hard to achieve his aims; an ancestor with a love of books and literature, who believed that education was both necessary and important if children were to develop and discover for themselves. I should like to think that I inherited similar pioneering qualities from this protagonist of education and literature from four generations back.

None of the members of his immediate family, however, showed any special love of books and learning, though one son, George, certainly displayed the spirit of adventure. George went to Chile, where he subsequently made a great fortune, coming to be known as the 'Chilean Nitrate King'. In later life George was outstandingly generous to his family. He eventually bought an estate called Murlingden, near Brechin, for his widowed mother and unmarried sisters. He also rented The Retreat, in the middle of Glen Esk, which has now been turned into a tea-room and museum. While I never ventured far afield physically, I did seem to possess a similar spirit of adventure in my pursuit into the unknown in quest of new methods of learning. In a lighter vein, the exploits of my childhood in the realm of bikes and motorbikes also seem to smack of the spirit of adventure, if not, indeed, of downright recklessness!

The Murlingden estate, however, came relatively late in George's career, after he had made his fortune. In 1858 David Inglis had died and his eldest son, also named David, had subsequently taken his wife, his mother and his brothers and sisters (including my grandmother, Catherine) to Weisdale in Shetland. The reason for such a move remains a mystery. In the natural course of things, the girls all married Shetland men with names such as Linklater, Robertson and Irvine. In 1879 Catherine herself married a Shetland farmer and the name Manson was added to the list.

She and William Manson, her husband, had a farm at Huxter, on the way to Scalloway, which was bleak in the extreme. It was there that the family of four boys and four girls grew up. My mother, Margaret Jane Clark Manson, was the eldest, being born in 1882. The children went to school at Weisdale, not far from Huxter.

Many years later I visited the school building, the journey by boat taking us across the end of the Weisdale Voe. By this time, however, it had been turned into a community centre, though an old school register had survived in a wall cupboard, still bearing the names of all the Manson family. They included that of my mother, Margaret Jane Clark Manson.

From all that I have been able to learn, my mother's girlhood in Shetland must have been simple, happy and extremely healthy. From time to time her mother used to travel to the mainland to visit some of her family who were still living in   Angus. On these occasions my mother, being highly domesticated, used to look after the house, the younger children, the cows, the sheep and no doubt part of the farm as well.

All this was brought to an end by the sudden death of her father, as a result of which the family returned to the mainland and set up house in Brechin once more. The two youngest of the children, Aggie and Willie, were still at school at the time. Of the elder ones, two went to New Zealand to farm, while the others took various jobs in Brechin. My mother, however, did not take a job and before long she had met and married one James Hollingworth, my father. As a young married woman faced with the task of making a new home for her husband and herself, she continued to develop her domestic talents, and especially her taste for colours, wood and furniture.

James Hollingworth was a Yorkshireman, born in a little village at Meltham, near Huddersfield. As far as I can remember, I never visited that part of Yorkshire, and the only relatives of my father whom I ever met were some delightful second cousins in America, who were particularly kind to me when I paid a visit there. Encouraged by my Yorkshire grandfather, both my father and his brother, my Uncle Harry, became accomplished musicians, my father playing the piano and organ and Uncle Harry the fiddle. In fact the brothers had come to Scotland to buy a music shop in Brechin which had been advertised for sale in a Yorkshire newspaper. This they proceeded to run jointly and it was in this way that my father came to meet and marry my mother.

In addition to giving lessons in the piano and flute, my father held the position of organist and choirmaster in the West Free Church. As a Yorkshireman, apart from his intense interest in music, he was also an avid cricketer. He played not only for the local Brechin team but for Forfarshire as well, being awarded his cap. The cap itself seemed to my child's eyes a miserable object. Coloured chocolate-brown with white circles, it looked like a mere scrap of material with a 'snout'. Nevertheless, I no doubt enjoyed playing with it.

Music, cricket and money-making – this strange combination of interests, typical of Yorkshiremen everywhere, were the overriding preoccupations of my father's life. He was fair, paid his debts, and always made sure that I did the same. One must keep one's accounts at all costs and never run into debt. These were lessons which I learned from him at a very early age. I remember him as constantly and intensely busy. When he was not teaching or working in the shop, he would be out tuning pianos, making his journeys to the surrounding countryside on what seemed to me then an enormous bicycle. I can see him now fastening his bicycle clips for just such a journey. He was highly popular; most people loved Jimmy Hollingworth and he would share a joke with all and sundry.

My mother was no less popular, enjoying jokes and happy parties and playing music herself. She could play tricks on people too, such as making them apple-pie beds, and this despite persistent ill-health, which necessitated frequent spells of convalescence at my grandmother's house. Like my father, she had a natural spirit of happiness, and I should like to think that this is a trait which, by good fortune, I have inherited from them both.

Although books and literature did not figure largely in our family home, I was brought up in an atmosphere of music. My father founded a Choral Society and an Operatic Society and acted as conductor in both. Hence all my life I have been familiar with the Gilbert and Sullivan operas and with the music of Handel. That type of music was my father's special love and as organist to the local choir he achieved great things for it. The love of music, therefore, being a prominent feature in my early background, played a major part in my subsequent life as well; here is a further characteristic which I must attribute to my father.

To explain my interest in literature, however, we must turn to my mother's side, though to her sister, Aunt Aggie, rather than to my mother herself. Aunt Aggie had a deep love of literature in general and of Shakespeare in particular even though she derived little encouragement in this from her own family circle, in which literature was not considered important. She also entertained and was very popular as a reciter. During the First World War she became a volunteer nurse and once it was over she married a farmer. That was the start of her deep love of horses, which became her whole interest. Together they bred beautiful hunters. The influence of Aunt Aggie upon me was profound; years later, when my mother was in favour of bringing me back from my training at the Royal Academy, she would invariably plead: 'Please let her finish, please let her qualify.' She was also outstandingly generous. In the letters she wrote to me while I was a student in London she would enclose a pound note. In many different ways therefore, financial as well as literary, Aunt Aggie was a major influence in my life. I miss that influence to this day, but most of all I miss her as a person.

Another aunt for whom I had a special affection was Aunt Jemima Manson, whom I always called Aunt Minja. She lived with my grandmother at St. Andrew's House next door to the High School in Brechin. The house itself is alas no more and I believe that it has been bulldozed. I remember her as a deeply kind person, but particularly as a fanatical cleaner, and this even though she had two people to help her. Her house always smelled of polish. She was a golfer and as I grew older we played together at Trinity and Edzell. It is as a walker, however, that I remember Aunt Minja most vividly. Together we used to explore the lovely city of Brechin, and one walk of which I have a clear recollection led down the Montrose Road and up by Leuchland, giving a particularly good impression of the city's special charms.

Yet another of my aunts was Aunt Mary. Apart from being an outstanding needlewoman, she was also very amorous! When she fell in love with a soldier of the Black Watch, I was dressed in a frock of the Black Watch colours which she made for me. When she transferred her affections to a sailor, I was dressed in a sailor suit and cap with the name of his ship – H.M.S. Neptune or some similar name – embroidered across it.

To this day I miss all three of these aunts of mine and I also miss my uncles. The youngest was Uncle William and if I was ever jealous of anybody it was of him. The reason for this was that he possessed a motorbike, something which I ardently desired; more of this, however, at a later stage in my story.

Let us return, however, to my parents and their married life together. Both, as we have seen, had backgrounds of hardworking, honest kindness and both were universally popular. In the light of all this it is astonishing to have to record that they were not suited to one another. My mother was devoted to the large Manson family in which she had grown up and retained a great affection for her own people; so much so that as I look back I feel that she never really cut the bond of her family ties and that she may even have put their needs before those of my father and myself. This perhaps explains the fact that so much of my early life prior to my schooldays was spent at my grandma's, Grandma Manson. She lived in East Bank Street, Brechin with her family, and it seemed to me delightful to have all the company there in their own family house.

Coming as she did from Shetland, my mother retained the lovely accent of the north and used Shetland words. I also remember her knitting in the Shetland way; she was so clever, so quick with her fingers. She was also a wonderful cook and baker, and when it came to sales of work or cake and candy stalls, Mrs. Hollingworth's sponge cakes were always the favourites. I have a vivid recollection also of her exquisite taste in colour, furniture and the shape of things, a talent which she could not have expressed amid the bleak conditions of the Shetland farm on which she was brought up, with its constant lack of money.

Meanwhile my father, preoccupied as he was with the constant need to make money in order to keep the family and the house, as well as with those two abiding loves of his, cricket and music, seemed to throw his whole life into these interests. Thus I was, to a large extent, left to steer my own course.

It seems significant now that my parents and I never once went on holiday together as a family. I would visit my grandmother's; my father would go off with one of my uncles or with friends. What my mother did I cannot remember, if indeed I ever knew. For her, I suppose, being on her own and having the freedom to do what she wanted was a holiday in itself.

In later life I remember one of my aunts remarking: 'You know, when you were a little girl, I never saw you in your mother's arms.' Certainly I have no recollection of any such experience, and I do remember how shy I always felt with my mother. When I went up to London for my studies, it was my father who took me. Yet my mother looked after me excellently and one of the gifts I value most from her has been the love of beautiful things which she taught me. The fact remains that I never really knew her in herself. What kind of woman she was – that I can recognise clearly: deeply kind, strikingly beautiful, exceedingly shy. Nor was I the kind of

                              Building Bridges

My Mother in her early twenties.

child she would have dreamt of or hoped for. In looks I took after my father and his side of the family and for my mother, as I now believe, the standards by which she assessed good looks were derived from those of her own family. Unfortunately I had none of them and with hindsight I now realise that a child is not slow to discover such attitudes.

All that, however, lies in the past. I can only regret the extent to which my relationship with my mother was destroyed, even though such an outcome was as far from her intention as from mine. I missed so much from her, as, I am sure, she did from me. That she did possess affection is certain, but so much of it was lavished on her Manson relatives, or else on her friends, her dogs, and particularly on her beloved hens.

One particular episode remains clearly imprinted on my mind, and it has a bearing on my relationship with my mother. It is, in fact, my only surviving memory of any social visit which I made in company with her. It was to Murlingden, the estate which, it will be remembered, Uncle George the 'Nitrate King' had bought for his widowed mother and unmarried sisters. It was a large, comfortable house built in local grey stone. By this time only my mother's aunt, Aunt Mary, was living there, with a cook and housemaid, and she had invited my mother to bring me to afternoon tea.

I was fully aware that our visit constituted a special occasion. When the time came to set out I was as clean and tidy as could be, with my hair shining in pretty gold curls. No doubt too, I had been specially told to remember my manners.

Murlingden lay about a mile and a half from Brechin and our route thither was later to become one of my favourite walks. It led out of the Cookstone Road, past the end of Maison Dieu Lane, past the cattle raik at the other side, and down the hill. At this point we turned in at the great gates and passed up the sweeping drive. To one side lawns stretched down to a lake with a little paddock beyond, while the drive itself was bordered by large rhododendron bushes. Being in full bloom, these made a striking sight. Finally we arrived at the imposing front door.

As the housemaid ushered us into the spacious hall, carpeted with deep, rich rugs, all was quiet; the only sound to break the silence was that of the grandfather clock. Round the walls hung large, gilt-framed pictures of race horses, copies, no doubt, of famous paintings. On the left rose the main staircase, its position to the side making it appear quite separate from the rest of the house. From the hall one could see right up to the ceiling above the first floor, which was decorated with the plasterwork typical of mansion houses of that period. At one end of the hall, just outside the dining room, stood a large sideboard of shining mahogany, while dotted here and there stood a few chairs, likewise shining with furniture polish. The whole was pervaded with the smell of beeswax, for everything – including the floor – capable of being polished was polished. To stand alone in that hall was enough to produce a tingling sensation in my spine.

From there we were ushered into the parlour to meet Aunt Mary. She was a proud woman, well built and always dressed in a black silk frock liberally embellished with black braid and with a loose pocket, also black, hanging from her waist.

The parlour was comfortably furnished and a fire glowed brightly in the grate. One wall was lined with well filled bookshelves while on another windows looked out on to the lake and paddock. I believe that Aunt Mary must have been in the habit of using the parlour as a small dining room, for at its centre stood a dining table. No doubt she would not have bothered to use the large dining room when she was by herself. For some time we sat there and then came the moment to which I had been looking forward: the moment when I could make a journey by myself across the big hall to the cloakroom which lay beyond. I asked to be excused.

As I crossed the hall and entered the cloakroom, I found that it was far darker. Right across the opposite wall stretched a mahogany screen. On opening this I found myself in the lavatory part, which was darker still, no sunlight being allowed to penetrate to it. To me the lavatory itself was unusual for it too was of mahogany and it extended over the entire width of the wall against which it stood. It was operated not by a chain or plug, but by a polished handle on the left side which had to be pulled up. The actual bowl was decorated with blue figures and may have been Wedgewood. To sit on the mahogany seat in the dark was an experience in itself. When I had finished washing my hands I re-emerged into the hall with its soft, beautiful rugs, its shining floor and furniture and its pregnant silence. Before returning to the parlour I paused there for a moment; it was my kingdom!

That was one of the happiest afternoons which I spent with my mother. All the way out to Murlingden I had been skipping, and now I skipped all the way back. From side to side of the road I skipped, neither walking nor running any part of the way. I was so happy! To be taken out by my mother must have been very special indeed. That was eighty-three years ago, yet the whole experience lives in my memory as vividly as if I were still a six year-old!

Chapter Two

Childhood Days

18 Bank Street – I was not born in that house, but soon after my birth in 1904, my parents set up home there. Hence it remains the centre of my childhood memories, the more so since it had so many features to delight and stimulate a child's imagination and provide a setting for imaginative games.

On either side of the house, reached by a flight of stairs, lay two large attics, one dark and sombre, the other full of light. On the first floor was a small room which was later used as a bedroom for the little maidservant who came to help my mother. Before that, however, it was my playroom and many of my early hours were spent in it.

All my play as a child was of the imaginative kind, and by no means exclusively confined to my little playroom; on occasion the dining room too provided scope for my creative spirit. Among other interesting objects, it contained a gramophone, one of the very old-fashioned types with a horn. Some of my father's records of classical music were also kept there; they included a particularly quick-moving piece called 'Zampa'. I used to wind the gramophone up, put the needle down and then, once the music was playing, become any one of a whole variety of characters. Sometimes I would be a shopkeeper and pretend to sell goods of various kinds – to myself of course!

I had to take all the parts in the scene I was conjuring up. Meanwhile the music would provide an excellent background and add to the atmosphere. To the front of the house, I remember a small piece of ground bordered by iron railings with the pavement just beyond. One day as I was playing there a friend of my grandmother's came across the street to speak to me. 'Hallo Cathie,' she said, 'What are you doing today? Which would you like, a penny or a banana?' I pondered a little. Then, 'I'll have a penny, please,' I said and duly received it. At that point I added: 'My golliwog likes banana skins!' That remark earned me the banana as well. Perhaps, therefore, there was something to be gained by all my imaginative play. Certainly the story entertained the family for a while.

I also remember vividly how strong a bond of affection existed between the animals of the household and myself. I have already mentioned how fond my mother was of them, and in this respect I was her equal. We had a beautiful Persian cat named Vickie and a black, white and tan Shetland collie named Billy. But my mother's special affection was lavished on the hens and she had names for every one of them. We kept them in a hen-run in the garden and I can remember her visiting the hen house and sitting for ages with one hen which was a particular pet. I, by contrast, was afraid of feathers and would not go near the hens. So great, in fact, was this fear of mine that when my father wanted to prevent me from taking my bicycle out by the back gate he used to hang a bunch of feathers on the gate handle. It was highly effective! So long as there was a bunch of feathers on the gate I would not go near it. Dead birds were even more frightening than live ones and the fear of feathers and feathered creatures persisted throughout my growing years.

Nevertheless, throughout my life I have never wavered in my love of animals and have retained the same warm affection for the numerous dogs I have owned that I experienced as a very small girl with Billy. The last of a long line of these dogs was a little fellow named Roy. He survived with us to the ripe old age of sixteen, by which time he was beyond the stage when he could enjoy walks. Even then, however, I only had to crawl along the floor to where he was lying and whisper 'walk' in his ear for him to be alert in an instant. He would not know which end of himself to get up first in order to go out. A point came when he was obviously no longer enjoying life and I decided that it was not fair to prolong it further. The vet came and he ended his days peacefully in my arms. He had been a highly active dog and would not have enjoyed the closing stage of his life. As one who has been highly active herself and is now forced, while retaining her mental faculties, to endure the loss of her physical powers, I feel deep sympathy with Roy.

My mother's family, the Mansons, continued to play a large part in our lives. At one time they lived at a farm near Fordoun called Pittengardner, a delightful place with a pond and a tree house overlooking it which, I believe, must have been built by my Uncle Willie. I retain vivid memories of climbing up to that tree house. When I was older, my father bought me a pony mare from Shetland and she was kept at Pittengardner. Though never broken in, she allowed me to ride her, though I was the only one who could. I called her Desdemona, a name inspired by a production of 'Othello' in the old City Hall at Brechin about 1913, to which Aunt Aggie, the youngest of my aunts, had taken me. The actress who played Desdemona was, to my mind, the most beautiful creature that I had ever seen in my life.

Inevitably, as an only child, I was alone for much of the time. However, both Aunt Aggie and Uncle Willie were still at school and were still young enough to have a certain affinity with me. That made it all the more fun to visit the farm as a change from the solitary life I led at home. I even have memories of being taken home screaming and crying after spending an afternoon and evening there with my young aunt and uncle. Even though many years their junior, I was so much happier in their company!

Being naturally observant and taking a delight in watching people, I became fascinated by the behaviour of churchgoers at the nearby church at Pittengardner, to which I was taken quite regularly. Among other things, I noticed how quietly the beadle used to enter with the great bible and how, in an aura of obsequious silence, he used to mount the stairs to the pulpit in order to place it there with the hymnbook on one side and the intimations on the other. Then he would withdraw, no less quietly, descending the stairs with his knees bending outwards, a gait which particularly struck my imagination. Finally he would stand waiting at the foot for the minister, Mr. Paterson, whose mode of entry would be in marked contrast. So hastily would he emerge from the side door that his gown, the white bands he wore over it and everything about him would seem to be flying. Then, the beadle having solemnly closed the door behind him, the minister would sit quietly down for a few minutes in the pulpit before standing to catch the congregation's attention.

So strong was the impression that this ritual made upon me that it became the inspiration for one of the games of imagination which I used to play at Pittengardner. I used to assemble my grandmother's four dogs, put them on a bed placed against a wall, and then fetch a chair with wooden handles, seat and back and set it in front of the bed. The play would then commence. I would go to the door and make my entry, copying the solemn walk of the beadle and carrying (though only with the utmost difficulty) the large family bible and other accessories. Approaching my improvised 'pulpit', I would pretend to mount the imaginary stairs and place my burden carefully in position. After that I would open the pulpit door and descend the stairs, faithfully copying the 'knees out' gait of the beadle as I did so, to await the arrival of the minister. Then it was time for a swift change of roles; I had to become the minister himself. Positioning myself at an imaginary side door, I would come rushing in with skirts flying, hurry towards the 'pulpit' and sit down. Then would come the climax: the moment when I had to catch the attention of the congregation. By this time, of course, the dogs would all be fast asleep on the bed. Nothing daunted, I would carry on with the hymns, the intimations, the reading from the bible, the sermon and finally the dismissal hymn. How I loved that hymn – I could play it now!

This reminds me of another incident connected with the same church. When I attended church it was invariably in the care of two ladies who lived nearby and were family friends. They were the Misses Mannings, Minnie the librarian and Lucy her sister. They lived just at the foot of Bank Street and on Sunday mornings I used to go down there, mounting a spiral stone staircase that led to their flat. They told me that as soon as their two cats heard my footsteps on those stairs, they used to scatter and vanish. That surely reveals something about me!

During the service Minnie, who used to stand next to me, would sing very vehemently, hanging on with one hand to the little rail that ran round the top of the pew while she held the hymnbook with the other. As she sang she would sway backwards and forwards. One particular Sunday I had taken a pack of cards from my pocket and was kneeling on the floor playing a game of patience on the green baize cushion. All was well until Minnie happened to look down and saw what I was doing. Then there was trouble! After that I was always asked: 'Have you anything in your pocket?'

When the time came for me to start going to school, I attended a kindergarten which had just been opened in Brechin by two ladies called the Misses Seivewright. Every morning I was taken to their school by a lady with long flowing locks, whose name was Beatrice Cockburn. Every time I hear the words of 'La Belle Dame sans Merci' I think of her. During the short period which I spent at this school I seemed to mix well with the other children. I was then promoted to Primary School, which was a branch of the High School, and here for the first time I found myself a member of large classes or, to be accurate, a single big Infant Department class presided over by a Miss Mitchell.

At this time a little boy named Gordon Stewart joined the school. His parents lived on a farm called East Mains of Keithock, near Brechin. He was unusually handsome and wore a kilt. Not long after his arrival, he told his mother that he was going to marry Cathy Hollingworth! How I came to find this out I cannot remember, but we certainly became classroom friends, visited one another's parents, and went right through school together until he was removed for not working and sent to Montrose Academy. I don't believe that I had any bad influence upon him, but certainly at the time I could see no sense in changing the existing arrangements. However, from Montrose Academy he went on to Edinburgh Academy, eventually becoming a chartered accountant in Dundee.

I was an unusually active child, and as soon as I could ride a small bicycle I was given one of my own. In retrospect I believe I must have been somewhat reckless. Bank Street lay on a very steep hill and the road, with its rough surface, was definitely bad – not a road which was easy for shoppers to drive on or even to walk along except by keeping to the pavement. We lived about half way down and I have vivid recollections of coming down the hill with my feet on the handlebars and my hands clutching handlebars and brakes together. I must have been lucky, however, for I cannot remember suffering any disasters.

One of the companions with whom I played at this time was a little girl named Babby Moir, who lived next door and was about my own age. Her father, I remember, was a railway guard. 'Are ye comin' out to play, Cathy?' she would sing and out we would go together. What particular games we played with our skipping ropes and balls I cannot recall, but Babby, like myself, was a girl of strong character, and we had to begin by coming to an agreement as to what those games were to be.

As we reached the top of Primary School we began to play hockey, even though we had no games mistress. Instead, our sports were presided over by a Sergeant Neish, a retired sergeant from some regiment or other, who used to bark out his orders to us as if we were army recruits. 'Get them thumbs on the side of your trousers!' he would shout, even though we never wore trousers! He was far too much of a terror for us ever to point out his error to him!

Away from Sergeant Neish's supervision, we mustered our own hockey team and played in the public park. Being quite a fast runner, I used to play as centre half for the team. We lacked both a proper pitch and a coach, yet somehow we managed to play.

By the time I had reached this stage in my life it was 1914 and the First World War had broken out. Nobody was playing tennis, for there were no men left and the women were all doing war work. In view of this, we were granted permission to use the tennis courts in Park Road, so we played tennis too. My uncles were all keen golfers and used to play initially at Trinity Golf Course and then at Edzell. So about this time I too began to play golf, acquiring a kit of small golf clubs of my own. In fact I often played with Gordon Stewart, who was both keen and outstandingly good at the game.

While at Primary School I became a Girl Guide, which proved very exciting – especially when I became the leader of the Blackbird Patrol. Whether any of the 'blackbirds' I knew are still flying I have no means of knowing, but I cannot suppose so. I may well be the only one left, and 'flying' is hardly the term to describe my present mode of ambulation!

The time I spent in the Girl Guides was particularly happy, even though I did have great difficulty in learning how to tie knots. The clove hitch was one that I could never manage, and in any case I could not see the sense in trying to learn. That apart, however, it was tremendous fun. We played games and worked for all the badges that were awarded to Girl Guides in those days.

Before leaving the Primary School I was awarded the 'Dux' Medal, otherwise known as the 'Smart' Medal. This latter name does not imply that it was given for smartness; rather, it was named after its donor, a Mr. Smart. Exactly what I had done to gain it I am not sure, but I suspect that it must have been a reward for being unusually aware of what was going on around me, and for having a gift for general knowledge of a kind, as distinct from factual knowledge or book knowledge.

At this stage, therefore, I was a keen Girl Guide, playing plenty of sport. Then a few years later a still more significant interest entered my fourteen year-old life.

As a new venture, the Girl Guides decided to do a play. 'A Midsummer Night's Dream' was chosen, and I was cast as Nick Bottom. Despite the fact that nobody knew much about drama, we were coached in our parts by the wife of the Rector of the High School, Mrs. Taggart, and were also helped by Miss Jo Lamb, who was well known for her music. Also included in the cast were Tibby, Mrs. Taggart's daughter, another girl named Eleanor, who played Puck, and her sister, who was a particular friend of mine. The actual performance took place in the garden of Miss Jo Lamb's house, which was called 'The Latch'. That was my first introduction to drama, and the part of Bottom could not have been a more delightful one with which to begin. I do not suppose I understood it all as well as I do now, but what is certain is that my lifelong love of acting received its initial spark on that summer's day in front of Miss Lamb's house.

At about the same period I was able to satisfy another long-standing desire of mine, namely to ride a motorbike. As I have already said, my Uncle Willie possessed one, the first of several which he acquired over the years, in this case a Matchless motorbike with side car. By this time my grandmother had given up the tenancy of Pittengardner and had just bought a house in Brechin called St. Andrew's House. Before the actual removal, Andrew, her chauffeur-gardener, had been coming to Brechin in the evenings to tidy up the new garden, using as his mode of transport Uncle Willie's motorbike. I, of course, had often ridden in the side car of that wonderful machine and had profited from my experiences by watching very closely to see how it was controlled. I had a clear knowledge of which buttons I needed to press.

One day I took the plunge. 'What about coming down to Montrose with me tonight in the side car?' I calmly suggested to my friend Jean Ferguson. She, for her part, never showed the smallest misgiving, so later that same afternoon we persuaded Andrew to lend us the motorbike, which at the time was parked in the driveway of St. Andrew's House. Accordingly, Jean ensconced herself in the side car, I mounted the bike and off we set, first down the lane, then along South Esk and Montrose Streets with all going smoothly. 'You know,' I remarked to Jean at this point, 'I thought this bike would go faster than this.' I actually wondered whether Andrew had retarded it in some way. I pressed every part of the controls I could see, and supposed I must have found the right knobs, more or less, for certainly it did give a sudden bound into a faster rate of proceeding. Down Montrose High Street we went and round the monument at the end. By this time I was beginning to wonder whether I could manage to stop the machine, let alone start it again once I had succeeded in doing so. I decided not to stop in Montrose after all; I would simply continue home, returning to Brechin by way of St. David's Street. At this point I espied, to my horror, my little cousin Marjorie standing on the pavement waving to us. Clearly she had recognised me. In itself that was not so bad, but subsequent events were to prove far more damaging. Up the lane and into the drive we went and I was able to stop the engine successfully enough. I had brought the bike home safely! Then I returned home, thinking no more about the matter.

Later that evening while sitting at table, Marjorie remarked, all innocence: 'Ah, Cath, I saw you in St. David's Street. You were on Uncle Willie's motorbike!'

'What?' exclaimed my mother, 'What's all this?' I had no recourse but to own up, and, as can be imagined, an unholy row ensued. Nevertheless a part of me remained unrepentant. While it lasted, it had been such an enormous thrill!

Another incident which must have caused some concern took place in the aftermath of one of my mother's 'at home' days. Whenever I think of those days they never fail to call to mind Mrs. Gaskell's 'Cranford'. In my mind's eye I can still see the ladies, adorned in Sunday hats and best clothes, arriving in our hallway, where they would leave their calling cards on a silver tray at the door. Each of them would have written on her card the day on which she in turn would be 'at home', so that Mother could return their visits. The cards having been duly placed on the tray, the ladies would make their way upstairs to the drawing room, where other ladies would already have assembled, to enjoy tea and cakes. There they would indulge in genteel talk while nibbling at my mother's excellent sponges and Madeira cakes tastefully displayed on the tiers of the cakestand, from which they would transfer them to plates of her best and most delicate china. The subject of their conversations must have been singularly lacking in interest to me, for I cannot remember any part of it.

For such 'at homes' I was, of course, always dressed in my best, and on one particular occasion this took the form of a 'coat frock', as it was called at the time. It was a lengthy garment fastened down the front and with long sleeves, which were cut particularly wide at the wrists. My task was to answer the bell, usher in my mother's guests, and provide such general help as I could, even though by that time the little country maid Bella was also there to assist.

A possession which my mother greatly prized, and which she used at her 'at homes', was a particularly fine Crown Derby tea service of dark blue with gold filigree. My father had built it up piece by piece over the years as a present to her. After this particular 'at home' was over and all the guests had left, I was carrying a tray of this china down to the scullery to be washed. Unfortunately, as I reached the door my wide sleeve caught the handle and the entire set went shooting off the tray. Although the floor immediately around me was carpeted, most of the cups, saucers and plates crashed against the hard door and the banisters of the stairway beyond. To put it mildly, the set was now no longer complete. Imagine my mother's feelings! Yet instead of raging or scolding me she simply said: 'Bury it in the garden – dig a hole and bury it!' In our garden stood an old plum tree which each year bore the most delicious Victoria plums. It was at the foot of this that, in accordance with my mother's instructions, I dug the grave in which most of the Crown Derby service was to be interred. Mournfully I emptied the broken fragments into it and shovelled the earth on top of them.

Next morning, however, my mother experienced a change of heart. 'We might see if we could glue the broken pieces together,' she said, 'Go and dig them up.' Once more I took the spade and did as I was bidden.

However, despite our best efforts to repair the broken china, it was all in vain. We no longer possessed a tea service. So much for my efficiency as an assistant at my mother's 'at homes'!

Soon after this episode a decision had to be taken as to whether I should continue at school any longer. One day my father made up his mind. 'I don't think you are going to do anything at school,' he said, 'You are too busy with your tennis, hockey and golf and with your Girl Guide activities. You have done nothing at all about your lessons and your reports always say: "Could do better." – I am going to send you to Dundee for elocution lessons, for elocution is the one branch of your education in which you seem to have some ability.' That was how I began my studies in elocution, travelling to Dundee to be taught by a lady named Rosa MacDougal, who had previously studied singing at the Royal Academy of Music.

As a result of this, I renewed my acquaintance with Gordon Stewart, who by this time was working in Dundee in a chartered accountant's office and living with his family in nearby Newtyle. As a result, we were able to spend many weekends together either at Newtyle or at my home. In the back of our minds we still retained our childhood idea that one day I should marry him. As it had survived for so long, my people, and even I myself, had come to accept it.

My secondary school education, therefore, was now at an end. Nowadays, when people ask me whether I was educated at Brechin High School, my answer is always the same: 'I went to Brechin High School, but my education didn't begin until I was about twenty-seven.' Elocution now became the dominant factor in my life and I was travelling to Dundee to be taught by Rosa, who proved an able instructor. I used to give recitations at W.R.I. clubs and similar institutions round about. At length a day came when Rosa gave me a letter to take to my father. When he had read it he said: 'Well, this tells me that you have some talent and that Miss MacDougal thinks you should go to the Royal Academy of Music in London, where they provide a good three years' training in elocution.' For my own part, I had never entertained the idea of embarking on such a course; I believed that I was to marry Gordon Stewart, and did not think much beyond the next day. My chief concern was whether it would rain or not and whether I would be able to play golf. One great advantage of golf, by the way, is that it can be played alone. Apart from my interest in this game, I used to do much walking and in the Brechin of those days I could go anywhere I liked accompanied by my dog – round Maison Dieu, for example, or over Burghill, or even right out to Cookston. One of my walks took me through Little Brechin, up by West Muir, and so home to Brechin. Another circuit led down the Montrose Road and back to Brechin by the same or a different route. Thus my time was largely divided between golf, walking and preparing for my lessons in Dundee. Now, however, I had much to contemplate on these walks of mine. Life was about to become quite different. I was going to London.

Chapter Three

In and Around London

In 1921, at the age of seventeen, I travelled to London to be interviewed by the Principal of the Royal Academy of Music, Sir Alexander McKenzie. The fact that I was a fellow Scot probably had an important bearing on his decision to admit me as a student, for otherwise I had little to recommend me.

After some discussion, it was arranged that I should take elocution as my principal subject with a Miss Newell as my teacher. A second principal subject would be the piano, which I would study under Marjorie Herman, and a third would be singing under the direction of Mary Wilson – six lessons a week all in all. In addition, I would study drama under Acton Bond, who had been one of Sir Henry Irving's players. I remember him as a fine looking man and a fine actor who was, of course, well versed in the classical plays. I also studied French under a Monsieur Thierry, who, on discovering that I was a Scot and as such had a better accent than most, took a special liking to me. He was in the process of becoming divorced and related to me in confidence the circumstances surrounding the matter. I believe it was I who actually posted his divorce papers!

One of my favourite subjects was fencing, in which I was instructed by a certain Madame Le Foy. She was a great character, attending lessons not in the usual fencing kit but in extremely high-heeled shoes, a red wig and a black frock with a very tight waist. As she entered she used to say: 'I 'ave been working with the opera. I am very tired, but not as tired as they are!' Just how tired they were, and how she would have put them through it, we could imagine. In all probability they would not have taken any real interest in dramatics as such, but under Madame Le Foy they would have had to put the most stupendous effort into their movement. I loved fencing and would have done more of it had sufficient time been available. So many hours had to be spent in practising, however, that keeping abreast of it all was very hard indeed: three hours a day at the piano, about one hour on singing and speaking, and, as if this were not sufficient, drama and French as well.

I enjoyed my lessons in singing and music, but never managed to derive much pleasure from the piano. The fact is that it was quite beyond me. Elocution I loved, even though I was beset by the problem of having a jaw that was far too stiff and rigid; that was one of the faults that had to be conquered first. A relaxed jaw, I learned, was a sine qua non. I remember having lessons from a Mrs. Tibas Mackie and also from a particularly able instructor named Irene Thomas.

On leaving me in London, my father had said to me: 'Well, Cath, now it is up to you.' That was something I never forgot, and I fully realised that it was at the cost of some sacrifice that my people were sending me to the Academy. In those days grants were non-existent, and no outside source of help was available. Nevertheless I was lucky in having my grandmother as well as my Aunts Aggie and Minja living in Berwickshire. In their letters to me they would always enclose a pound or ten-shilling note. I was all the more grateful for this since my parents never seemed to realise how much everything cost in the metropolis, and that it was impossible to walk everywhere. One had to take buses. It was a far cry from Brechin!

During my sojourn in London my only treat – and it was a treat indeed – was to go to Fullers with a small group of fellow students on an occasional Saturday afternoon to have walnut cake and coffee. Even that depended on whether we had enough money at any particular time.

I spent three years in all at the Royal Academy and as I look back I realise how privileged we were. For example, the conductor of the student orchestras was Sir Henry Wood, and we had access to any of their rehearsals in the Duke's Hall as and when we liked. Invariably we would find it full of students who were either waiting to attend a class or had come in specially to watch Sir Henry conducting. How often I have seen him use his baton to knock the music irately out of the hand of somebody who was attempting to sing but failing to keep to the rhythm. The soloists must have found such occasions completely nerve-wracking.

I found digs at Hillthorpe Crescent with a family who had lived in Auchenblae and was known to my people. Incidentally, at one time Crippen the murderer had lived in that neighbourhood, though not, I hope and believe, in the same house!

As far as I can remember, the round of study and homework that had to be completed left no time for any other occupations. In fact I had to work very hard indeed. I had no hobbies and golf was most certainly 'out'. I did, however, spend one or two weekends with one or two of my fellow students – one who lived in Essex and another, Nora Bennett-Lynch, who gave me invaluable help. She lived in Winchmore Hill, where I often spent my weekends. In later years, when I went to London on business, that was where I would stay. Apart from these two, I hardly came to know anyone very well, and in any case would never have had the time to make any other close friendships. In the end, however, it was all worth the effort. At the termination of my course I passed all the examinations and was awarded my L.R.A.M. There was even mention of a sub-professorship, though I failed to realise the importance of that and felt no particular interest in it; I still had no intention of involving myself in this type of work permanently. The idea of a career never entered my mind. Instead of bending myself to seize the chance I seemed to have been offered, therefore, I ignored it and confined myself to completing my three years' training.

When I returned to Brechin I soon found that the position of elocution teacher simply did not exist and that no demand for such teachers existed either. The ability to speak was something that the people of Brechin took for granted, failing to recognise any relevance which the teaching of elocution might have to their lives. In Dundee Miss Dougal had been first and foremost a teacher of singing, and of speech only in an entirely secondary sense. Yet here was I offering speech training only. I had concentrated on learning how to speak and how the human voice should be produced, but no one saw any relevance in that. Here I was then, ready to undertake whatever work might turn up. By this time, however, the quest for a job was not particularly urgent for me. Gordon had gone to India, whence he was regularly writing to me and making plans for me to join him in Madras.

At this juncture the headmistress of St. Margaret's School for Girls in Aberdeen invited me to adjudicate at their festival of poetry-speaking. I accepted and found the experience thoroughly enjoyable. So far as I can remember, the upshot was that, to my joy, I was engaged as a part-time elocution teacher at the school, working there three days a week. This continued for three years, during which I used to travel to and from Brechin daily by car.

Meanwhile in Brechin itself I had another job to occupy me. I was organising teams of actors and producing plays for the Girls' Club there.

We used to put on concerts, short plays and performances of folk singing. These always needed an accompanist on the piano and my father most willingly fulfilled that role. I, of course, always called him 'Dad' and gradually all the girls came to do the same, which he loved.

A great spirit of happiness pervaded the Girls' Groups. A strong feeling within me told me that unless we could establish a bond of mutual effort between the players and myself, our attempts in the field of drama were doomed to failure. The experience of working at producing plays with these groups was highly valuable and I learned much from it that was to stand me in good stead in my later work.

I remember particularly one comment made years later by a former member of the Girls' Club: 'When I was a girl in Brechin there were only two classes of people: the 'up the tooners' and the 'doon the tooners', and if you were nae ony o' them and ye *are* nae ony o' them – fit are ye then?' As a comment it was highly interesting. My activities were never prompted by any particular underlying belief or ideal; I did what I did because it was a happy, creative thing to do and I was doing it with a group of people who, whatever their background, enjoyed working together.

At this time too I was producing for the Forfar Dramatic Club and at the Scottish Community Drama Association Festival we put on a play about a coal miner. The occasion was somewhat momentous for we actually won! This despite the fact that neither I nor any of the players knew anything about coalmining! Under the circumstances, to have won first prize in Scotland was quite a coup! Unfortunately the Club was not affiliated to the British Drama League, so it could not proceed to even greater glories. However, what made the production especially interesting was that the cast was invited to perform it on radio. Our crowning satisfaction was to receive a letter from the play's author, Joe Corrie, who wrote to me to say that he had never expected to hear his play portrayed so truthfully.

Eventually I became involved with a whole range of drama groups throughout Angus, at such locations as Kirriemuir and Ruthven. So much was I occupied with all this that I decided to terminate my appointment as visiting teacher at St. Margaret's. However, years later I was to return to the school as a resident teacher, living in the boarding house at Queen's Gardens. This, however, was only after many other experiences in the intervening years.

In 1927 a fresh opportunity arose quite out of the blue and completely unconnected with any of my existing work. I was invited to become a member of the Summer Players. This was a group of young professional women who had a special interest in drama and music. During the month of August they used to meet in Perthshire at the strikingly beautiful house of Dr. Katherine Briggs, where they used to perform plays, sing folksongs and recite poems. Needless to say, I at once accepted the invitation and for a fortnight we worked together at Dunkeld rehearsing such songs as 'The Raggle Taggle Gypsies' and 'Dashing Away with the Smoothing Iron'. I was the singer while the others acted the songs. It was just as well that I had a good clear voice and had the advantage of a training in singing. Although I could never have been a professional singer, I could sing distinctly and this was important, because in these performances, apart from the words I sang, no others were used. We had a fine pianist, who also played the dulcimer.

In addition to songs, we performed plays, many of them written by Dr. Briggs herself. She had been a scholar of Lady Margaret Hall, Oxford and was well versed in folklore. After the fortnight of rehearsals at her house, we would go on tour to various parts of Scotland. One year we even went as far as Somerset and Dorset. We were always given hospitality by the people to whom we were performing. One night we would be 'put up' by the lady of the manor, the next by the postmistress or the keeper of the village shop. We would go wherever we were put.

That summer visit to Somerset and Dorset was particularly memorable to me. It was a part of the country that was all new to me and it was so beautiful and enjoyed so marvellous a climate that I fell in love with it. All morning we would rehearse and in the afternoons we used to go for walks on the Quantock Hills, always seeming to stop somewhere for cream teas.

In all this our major financial benefactors were the family of Dr. Briggs – coalmine owners from Leeds, I believe. Though they did not pay us wages, they made themselves responsible for any expenses we incurred. One such expense was costuming, but it was dealt with in a particularly clever way. We used to play in either medieval or eighteenth-century costume and for the latter used to add ruffs or lace ruffles round the neck and sometimes at the cuffs. Wigs and loose jackets and waistcoats were used to complete the outfit.

In this connection, one experience of mine while in Dorset proved highly embarrassing. I discovered that my mother's cousin and his wife lived very near, so it was arranged that they would give me hospitality. Accordingly, having arrived at their house, I changed into my medieval costume before going down to dinner. Not knowing these people very well, I was already feeling a little nervous and made matters worse when a piece of toast which I had broken went skidding off across the polished table. My self-consciousness intensified when I came out to the hall after dinner. I found that the butler had taken every coat and hat out of the back of the little car I was driving and had laid them all on a big chest in the hall. I should explain that these were the coats and other garments in which we picnicked in the fields. Many of them belonged to other members of the company, who had thrown them in the back of the car for safety. 'Which one will you wear, Madam?' the butler enquired in pompous tones. My embarrassment can be imagined!

What happy, carefree days those were! We were quite independent, carrying our own lighting, music, props and costumes with us as we travelled round the country performing for Women's Institutes in England and Women's Rural Institutes in Scotland.

I worked with the Summer Players every year until 1933 and I believe that it was among them, with their marvellous conversations on such topics as literature, music and history, that my true education was initiated. In the Briggs' household these things mattered. My love of books and my acquisition of them date from those days. Every book I bought I loved; to me it became a precious jewel in a crown or necklace. As a purchase I had to make sure that it was worthwhile and that I could afford it, for even in those days books were expensive. Yet over the years, from 1927 onwards, I gradually gathered hundreds of them: works of literature, literary criticism, fiction, a large collection of poetry as well as specialist works on speech therapy. How much books meant to me I never realised until two years ago, when the time came for me to sell my flat and I was forced to let them go. By that time I had eighteen feet of bookshelves, the contents of which were more valuable to me than clothes, jewels or any other possible possessions. Possessions as such I have never valued, but books – that is a different matter! Now I realise what a loss these are to me, even though, having become blind, I have to depend on the spoken word.

I continued with the Summer Players up to 1933. Then came an event momentous enough to have a profound effect on the rest of my life.

Chapter Four

Speech Therapy

In 1933 I had a fairly nasty road accident. While driving to Kirriemuir I crashed into a lorry carrying tons of granite chips. My face was torn from the corner of my ear to the part below the middle of my lip, and the muscle connections to my lips on the left side were severed. As a result, I found myself unable to form the lip movements used for sounds such as 'ooh', 'oh', 'th' or 'f'. I did have the advantage of my elocution training to help me, and knew how sounds were made. Hence I was able to help myself to a far greater extent than would otherwise have been the case. Nevertheless, the disability meant that I had to give up teaching elocution.

While I was recovering in Brechin, a Mrs. McCormack came to see me with her little boy, Jock. 'My son has a very bad stammer,' she said, 'and I believe you know quite a lot about speech. Could you help him?' At the time I actually believed, in my ignorance, that I did know something about stammering. Moreover I was more than willing to be of service to anyone. Accordingly I said I thought I might be able to help the little boy.

Once I had visited him at his home in Montrose Street, however, I soon realised how ignorant I was on the subject. Nothing daunted, I borrowed all the literature on stammering that I could find in libraries and tried to learn what to do. At that time speech therapy as a branch of the therapeutic skills was very little known. I did discover that it was concerned with the rehabilitation of speech after breakdown, and that stammering was a prime example of such a breakdown. I also learned that the London County Council ran classes for stammering children, so I wrote to the Medical Officer of Health for London asking whether I could come and see what was being done in the field of speech therapy.

Any initiative of this kind which I took had of course to be carried out at my own expense, and here Nora Bennett-Lynch, my friend from Royal

31

Academy of Music days, showed herself truly helpful by asking me to
stay with her while I was in London.

It was in August that I made my trip, and once I arrived it was not long
before I was astonished and fascinated to discover speech therapy. I made
contact with those who had influence in the field at the time, including a
Miss Richardson, who was in charge of the London County Council Clinics. These were clinics held in the schools, in which emphasis was laid on
the importance of total relaxation. During a typical clinic the pupils of the
school involved, both boys and girls, would begin by taking their own mats
and pillow slips, together with cushions, from the wall cupboards of the
room where the clinic was being held. Then they would lie down on their
mats and the teacher would start to give them practice in systematic
relaxation, beginning with the toes and slowly working through all the
groups of muscles up the body to the top of the head. This was followed by
visual relaxation, which consisted in concentrating on a quiet and peaceful
scene. The aim of this was to relax all muscles to the fullest possible
extent. Relaxation was, I found, particularly important for those with
stammers, since stammering is characterised by extreme muscle spasm and
tension. Naturally, in the sixty years which have elapsed since those days,
the therapy has greatly changed, but that is how it was conducted then.

I spent a month in London, and so interested and enthusiastic did I
become about speech therapy, that I formed the ambition of taking it up as
a profession. On my return home, however, when I asked my father
whether I could train to become a speech therapist, his answer was a
decided negative. He had already paid for my training in speech, drama
and elocution, he said, and was not prepared to do any more. I set myself
to discover a solution to the problem. I knew that this was a true profession and that with it I would eventually be able to achieve a sufficient
income to finance myself. However, if I were ever to achieve my aim, I
would certainly have to leave Brechin. Once more, therefore, I packed my
bags and books and set off back to London to stay with Nora at
Winchmore Hill.

Since I wanted to obtain a complete training in speech therapy, I now
deliberately made contact with those involved in hospital – as opposed to
school – therapy. One of my contacts was a certain Eileen McLeod, who
was then at King's College Hospital in Denmark Hill. Having achieved an
entree there, I was able to profit from the amenities of an excellent clinic.
The space available was divided into three main parts: an office section, a
large waiting room well equipped for children and adults, and a part
which might have been described as a laboratory. This was my first

experience of what well organised accommodation should be and years later, when I had to organise similar accommodation in Aberdeen, it was to prove invaluable. During my stay in London I also worked at the Ear, Nose and Throat Hospital in Fitzroy Square, and studied anatomy and physiology with private tutors.

To pay for all this I was able to take advantage of the qualifications in elocution and drama which I had obtained from the Royal Academy of Music. I taught evening classes in speech and drama under the auspices of the London County Council and in addition took a job with the Municipal College at Southend-on-Sea. This work brought in sufficient money for me to maintain myself and pay for the private tutoring, and I was also able to undertake voluntary work in speech therapy.

Southend-on-Sea is a very long way from London – at least it seemed so in those days. On my journey there, however, I could enjoy one major treat, namely the hot chestnuts which could be bought from a vendor at Liverpool Street Station. I can still see his charcoal fire glowing through the darkness and smell the trayful of chestnuts resting on the top. On my return from Southend after work, I invariably succumbed to the temptation of buying a bag (they cost about twopence!) and, tired as I was, those chestnuts were absolutely delicious. Sometimes the buses were delayed by fog, so that I had to wait a long time at Liverpool Street. At such times I simply sat and ate my chestnuts until I could continue my journey home.

Eventually I found myself able to move into a little flat in Gower Mews, just off Gower Street and behind Tottenham Court Road. One day, as I was working at the Ear, Nose and Throat Hospital, one of the surgeons, a Mr. Jones, asked me if I could take a patient of his. I had to point out that my place was not exactly on a par with his surgery in Queen Anne Street next to Harley Street. 'Oh,' he replied, 'I only come up here a couple of days a week. You can have my rooms at any other time.' Accordingly, though with some trepidation, I accepted his offer and found myself working in a handsome West End house. However, there was more to it than this. To my horror, I found that the amenities included a butler. He used to ring me up and say: 'Your patient awaits you, Madam.' I found this quite terrifying until I discovered that he himself had a son with a stammer. From then on we had frequent talks about how the boy could be helped, and I relaxed far more. By this time I was thoroughly and happily embarked on my chosen course of training to become a speech therapist. The only part I did not like was the necessity of having to present my clients with their bills, yet it was vital in order to maintain myself. If I did need more money, I could take on additional work on the drama side.

All was going well and happily, therefore, until the disruptions occasioned by the outbreak of war in 1939. Immediately all those in a position to do so vacated London. Many of the outpatient clinics closed, and as the children were evacuated the school clinics did the same. The Queen's College Hospital Clinic was also shut down in order to make room for the wounded who were expected back from the war zone.

Nora and I decided to join the Women's Land Army, an extraordinary step to take in view of the fact that neither of us was really accustomed to hard work on the land. However soon afterwards I received a letter from Aunt Aggie, the aunt who was interested in literature and who had married a farmer. She suggested that since we were joining the Land Army we might as well come to work for her and her husband on their farm, Auchenrow Mains in Berwickshire, an offer which we gladly accepted.

Auchenrow Mains was a delightful and well-run farm not far from the town of Berwick. My uncle bred horses there and my aunt too was a keen horsewoman. However, unlike her husband and daughter, she never liked hunting. We spent the early part of the war working on the farm and living in very comfortable accommodation in the farm house. Sometimes when the work was particularly hard we would be joined by my aunt herself. One of the most arduous tasks, I believe, was that known as 'shawin' baigies'. This entailed clearing the ground of the tops of turnips which the sheep had munched. To pick up the half-consumed turnips we used special tools shaped somewhat like pickaxes but with a sharper end. Meanwhile the sheep would have been fenced off from the area we were clearing and when we had finished they would be turned back in to eat up the remains we had collected. As we continued with our careers in the Land Army the work seemed to become harder and harder. We spent six whole weeks working with the potato crop and on returning to the house for lunch we used to strip and rub some form of embrocation into our aching backs.

Of course the life was not without its lighter moments. We started a little drama group and here the material that had been used by the Summer Players came in very useful for the small group we had mustered. Probably that was the most enjoyable part of our stay in Berwickshire, not only for us but for Aunt Aggie as well for, having always been a great lover of literature and the arts, she used to join in too. As I have said, she was a great horse lover and I shared this love with her. In the early mornings before breakfast we used to exercise the horses, walking them carefully along the roadsides in the frost. On returning, I often found myself having to eat my breakfast from the dining room mantlepiece; sitting down would have been far too painful!

I continued working in Berwickshire until I was allowed to return to Brechin on compassionate grounds. My mother became very ill and I stayed with my parents until she had recovered. Meanwhile I was again undertaking a little work with the Girls' Club in Brechin.

By this time the scar left from my road accident had completely closed over and healed and the difficulties I had had with my speech had been all but eliminated. I had also attained my qualification in speech therapy. My next step, therefore, was to look for work in this field. The nearest place to Brechin where any such work was available was the Child Guidance Clinic in Dundee, where a particularly fine educational psychologist named Dr. Agatha Bowley was working. I arranged to do voluntary work under her in a clinic in Dundee Training College on the understanding that Dundee Town Council was shortly to appoint a speech therapist and that I would stand a very good chance of being accepted for the post. My plans in this direction, however, were not destined to come to fruition.

By this time I had become what is sometimes known as a 'workaholic' and this had become an obstacle to any thoughts of matrimony which I might have entertained. Gordon Stewart was now in Bangalore and my engagement to him was broken off. Eventually he married a colonel's daughter there. I often wish that he could have known how much more happiness I was to find in the course my life had taken. I would have made a very bad memsahib and would have been useless to him. As it was, I lost touch with him and never saw him again.

PART II. BUILDING BRIDGES

'The more bridges you know about, the more places you can see.'

Arnold Wesker

Chapter Five

The 'Speech Wifie' in Aberdeen

By 1940 my plans had changed again. I had returned to St. Margaret's School in Aberdeen, this time as a resident teacher. In the following year Aberdeen Town Council advertised for a 'Teacher of Speech'. With my knowledge of elocution, speech therapy and drama, I felt qualified enough, but was intrigued to know what the post would actually entail. When I made enquiries, however, I found that the authorities were reluctant to specify which aspect of speech training they had in mind. For my part I was not really interested in the post; by now my overriding ambition was to work as a speech therapist with patients needing rehabilitation; those, for instance whose speech had been impaired by strokes or who had undergone operations for cancer of the larynx. Other cases too of speech impairment associated with medical conditions would need therapeutic help. My father's advice, however, was: 'If you get the offer of that job, you had better take it.'

Duly heeding these words of his, I applied for the post. Five other women had also applied, all of them very well known in Aberdeen, and I thought I had little chance against them. To my surprise, however, it was I who was appointed. The fact that I was qualified in speech therapy as well as in what was then called elocution told, I suppose, in my favour, but in the course of my interview one point was made clear. The Education Committee was not looking for a speech therapist. Once I embarked on the job, therefore, I would always make it clear to those concerned that my role was not that of a speech therapist. At the same time, I would make it no less clear to the Education Committee that a speech therapist was sorely needed. In time they actually heeded my message and appointed one. That, however, lay in the future; let us return to 1941.

I began by calling upon the Director of Education for Aberdeen in order
to achieve a rather more detailed picture of what my new job would entail
and what he was actually seeking to achieve. 'Quite honestly,' he said, 'I
don't know, but we want the children to be more confident in speaking.
They seem to be quite happy so long as they are using their own dialect
but in the presence of anyone who doesn't speak that dialect they are
reduced to shyness and total silence. We want someone to help them with
that particular aspect. You had better go round the schools, get to know
them, get to know the different types of classes and children, and make
your plans accordingly.'

It was extremely good of him to give me that degree of freedom. No
actual Department of Speech Training existed, and I was the sole 'Teacher
of Speech'. It is interesting to note that in defining my role the word
'elocution' was never used. In advertising the post, the Aberdeen Education Committee had avoided the term because they were enlightened
enough to realise that the teaching of phrases such as 'how now brown
cow' and 'the rain in Spain' was not the approach they wanted and would
not achieve the aims they had in mind. Nowadays, of course, the term
'elocution' is no longer employed; in the late 1940s it was replaced by the
twofold description, 'Speech and Drama'.

What my salary was I cannot now remember, but it was certainly not
large. Never having qualified at a teachers' training college in Scotland, I
was not at that stage recognised as a teacher. Nevertheless, I had to belong
to a Trade Union. I therefore joined N.A.L.G.O., the National Association
of Local Government Officers, and for the first year or two it was to the
category of 'Local Government Officer' that I was assigned.

My remit then was clear and it amounted to a challenge. It did not fit
into any of the normal categories, namely elocution, speech therapy or
drama. At the same time, with this tremendous freedom to work in the
schools came a responsibility which was no less tremendous and which
was all the more awe-inspiring since my appointment was new and un-
precedented. It gave rise to much discussion among those concerned with
education. 'Why do we need someone to teach our children to speak?'
many teachers would say, 'They speak perfectly well already.' Many
indeed, head teachers as well as teachers, viewed the creation of the post
with disfavour. Being aware of all this, I had to tread extremely carefully.
Nevertheless, I usually got on with people quite easily and, with a judi-
cious admixture of humility, managed to make positive communication
with them. That did not, of course, involve playing the role of Uriah
Heep! Humility in this context meant that I was not representing myself as

the person with all the answers. Far from this, I adopted the attitude of someone who had come to learn, with the help of head teachers and teachers, to cope with the problems in my field. The capacity to take such an attitude was something which, I believe, I had learned from my mother.

When I first went into Primary Schools I had to teach entire classes. When trying to encourage effective speech, that is a very hard way of going about it. Basically communication consists of a confrontation between two individuals. Since classes in those days could amount to as many as forty, the situation was not exactly conducive to effective learning. Again, the teaching methods of the time were not particularly helpful. 'Now, take out your books and pencils and copy this off the blackboard,' the class teacher would often say, or 'Write down what I say.' Such an approach does nothing to encourage the individual pupil to make progress in speaking confidently or fluently. Here then was a major problem for me.

A further problem was the need to create an ambience in which the children could be happy and relaxed and in which I could establish a relationship with them. In the classrooms of those days fear was a considerable factor, and by no means all of them could generate an atmosphere of trust and encouragement. In this respect, I found, I had a second major task to achieve.

From the outset I had to establish clearly in the children's minds what I was trying to do with them and why. One factor which proved invaluable in my work was the firm foundation in the essentials of speech which had been laid down by my training at the Royal Academy of Music. Speaking, after all, is an activity in which certain muscles have to be put to work to make the sounds needed to form words for the listening ear to receive. Hence it is essential to achieve an understanding of what has to happen in order to make this activity come alive.

To the children this approach to language was entirely new. In fact they had never thought about language in terms of speech; so far as they were concerned, it had always been embodied in the written word. Seldom did they have occasion to speak to their teacher except in answer to a question, when their replies would be couched in a short phrase or even a single word. Now they delighted in being allowed a greater opportunity to express themselves orally.

I showed them that mumbling and indistinct speech is due to a failure to use the lips, tongue or jaw. Once I had illustrated this, they agreed that whoever was speaking, it was embarrassing for the listener to have to keep saying, 'Beg pardon'. Mumbling, therefore, made communication extremely difficult and yet it was so widespread. By actually speaking in a mumble, I was able to provide a vivid illustration of the point to them and they would see the practical commonsense of what I was trying to do.

Sometimes at the beginning of a class I would carefully refrain from using my tongue. Afterwards I would ask: 'Can you tell me which muscle I was not using properly?' At first they would find it difficult to identify the particular muscle concerned, but at least they would be motivated to try to discover the answer and I would continue until they did. It might be the tongue, one or other of the lips, or both, or it might be the jaw. All these points they quickly learned to spot. Then, of course, they tried it out for themselves. From there we would move on to all sorts of oral activities which were suitable for the particular age of the class concerned.

The age group that I found most intimidating was the 'Infants'. I found it necessary to devise special ways of working with them, and in the course of time this led me to develop different methods for different age groups. I do not want to give the impression that this was achieved in a moment. On the contrary, it was a gradual process, built up over a long period. It took me hours to prepare my lessons. When I returned to my 'digs' after work, I would have my evening meal and then spend the whole evening analysing what had worked or not worked, as the case might be, and why it had worked with one age group and not with another. In the case of the infant groups, the maximum length of my classes would be half an hour, yet it is an interesting fact that I would have spent several hours, or even several evenings, in their preparation.

For these infants, a rich store of material in the form of nursery rhymes lay ready to hand, and I used it for all types of work. At the commencement of a class I would say: 'Now, in a moment I am going to make some words, but they won't have any sound in them from here. I will use only the tools.' Then we would have a little talk about 'tools'. What were tools? Who used them? What were the tools a person used with which to speak? To questions such as these the children would respond readily and spontaneously; they loved trying to answer them. Thus if I 'lipped' a nursery rhyme they would watch as though their lives depended on it and they became extremely quick and adept at spotting which it was. Alternatively, I might deliberately refrain from using my lips properly, whereupon they would discover how much more difficult it was to spot the nursery rhyme. Thus they came to realise that if they were going to achieve distinctness in their speech they would have to use all the speech organs. At the same time they found that it was actually fun to do so.

The factor of dialect could, of course, have been an obstacle. At first many of the children thought that I was English, but by speaking some Scots to them I soon made it clear that I was a Scot like themselves. To illustrate the point, I would sometimes use a piece of poetry, for instance, one from William Souter's book, *Seeds in the Wind* or some similar piece. One poem which I used regularly, and which seemed to entertain the children at the same time as conveying my message was the following:

Wee Wullie Wagtail,
Whit is a' yer stichie?
Tak' a sup o' watter
An' cowrie o'er the steinn.

Ilke tree stans dozit
An' the wind wi'oot a hishie
Flitters in atween the floors
An' shaugs them ane by ane.

At this my pupils would be absolutely baffled! 'What language do you think that was?' I would ask. German, some of them thought; others would plump for some other foreign language; no one ever said Scots. In the end, when I told them, I would explain that that was how Scottish people in Auchterarder, Perthshire, would speak. After that I would recite a poem in their own dialect so that they could hear the difference. Then I might recite a poem in a mumble, making no effort at clear enunciation and reducing it to dull lifelessness. Again it illustrated how important it was to use the speech organs properly, whatever the dialect might be.

The place of dialect in education has been the subject of much controversy, some experts contending that it should never be used, others that everyone should be able to speak at least one dialect. My own view is that speech is one of the greatest gifts – if, indeed, not the greatest gift – that man possesses. Certainly it is the most powerful means of communication, others being gesture and the written word. Speech, however, is unique in its directness and, in a world where communication takes place between people of all types, from all sorts of places and in every variety of situation, it must surely be made as easy as possible to listen to and understand. It follows that what is needed is a form of English which can be understood by anyone who speaks the language at all. Only so can it be a useful and practical means of communication. Side by side with this, children should, I believe, also be able to speak their own dialect, but even then it should be clearly enunciated.

Unfortunately the subject of dialect is too often submerged in sentimentality. The fact remains that whether it be in the Doric, the received pronunciation or in a foreign language such as French, slovenly speech is slovenly speech! Indeed, to speak good Scots effectively requires a major effort. It is a strong, vigorous language and makes the speech muscles work hard. By way of example we may take the words of the twenty-third psalm written in Scots by Douglas Young:

> 'The Lord's my 'herd,
> I shall nocht want.
> He gars me doon to lie
> Whaur fresh, sweet burnies rowe . . .'

To mumble that is to destroy its inherent vigour and clarity. The twenty-third psalm is a splendid piece of literature in itself, but I must confess to preferring Douglas Young's translation of it into the Scots.

To return, however, to speech education in those early days. In order to achieve my aims, I found myself having to invent a whole range of fresh approaches. Even at that stage I was already using dramatisation as a device with the infants. While reciting the words of 'Little Miss Muffet', for example, we actually played the part of Miss Muffet or the spider as we spoke.

As I embarked on my teaching in the Primary Schools, this, as I remember, was how I found my way. Individuals are still living who can recall those first attempts of mine. A case in point is a lady from one of the voluntary aid associations in Aberdeen who came to visit me only the other day. 'I knew who I was coming to see,' she remarked, 'because you came to teach our class in 1943. I remember because I enjoyed it so much.' After fifty years that lady recalled not only the experience itself but the enjoyment she derived from it as well. I always considered that enjoyment is one of the main and most vital ingredients in any success one may achieve with children.

Before long I became known as 'the speech wifie', and it was a label to which I became accustomed. I might be walking up the Gallowgate to go to St. Margaret's Episcopal School or perhaps to Causeway End or even right on to Hanover Street. Wherever it was, as soon as the children in the playground caught sight of me they would come rushing across. 'Here's the Speech Wifie!' they would proclaim to all and sundry. Before I knew it, there they would all be, clustered at the other side of the railings. I loved it! How I appreciated the open, friendly welcomes I received wherever I went. In very truth I was Aberdeen's 'Speech Wifie'.

Chapter Six

Speech in the Classroom

The work I had now embarked upon was new and exploratory. Under the circumstances, it seemed only commonsense to make contact with other cities to find out what they were doing in the field of speech training and to obtain advice as to how to proceed. It was then that I discovered that no department of speech training as such existed anywhere else in Britain; we were on our own. As time went on and the work load increased, more members of staff were appointed and as the staff grew, so did the activities.

About this time, though quite accidentally, I discovered a fresh tool with which to encourage the spoken word; it was the use of puppets. One morning my friend Alice Taggart and I attended a lecture on the subject of puppetry. At the end she turned to me and said: 'You know, I think I could make these things.'

Though I had never thought of myself as a puppeteer, I found her suggestion both surprising and intriguing. We obtained a few books and a quantity of materials, with the result that before long she was making the most exquisite puppets. So great was her gift in this new field that eventually she was supplying Hamley's, the famous toy shop in London's Regent Street. A time came, however, when Hamley's decided to replace her beautiful handmade puppets with commercially manufactured ones. Nevertheless she continued to make them for me and I continued to find them invaluable in my speech training throughout the entire range of groups with which I was engaged.

While Alice was making her puppets, I was beginning to master the skills of working them. I should explain that most of the time we used glove puppets, because with them it is so easy to use the hands for such parallel purposes as picking things up and putting them down, clapping and so on. A possible drawback, however, is that usually they have no legs. For my first visit to an infant school I had asked Alice to make puppets for dramatised versions of 'Goldilocks and the Three Bears' and 'The Tale of a Turnip'. From the outset these proved a major success, and puppetry became a valuable, as well as a highly enjoyable, part of the work of the Department. Later we used puppets for a performance of 'The Insect Play', and these again were specially made for us by Alice Taggart. In the course of time we built up a stock of puppets which could be used for infant, primary or secondary schools, for establishments of further education and even for groups of adults. We also had a puppet theatre, which would have been about eight feet high. It was equipped with a backcloth so arranged, with the lights in front, that while we could see the audience through it, they could not see us. Everyone loved the puppets, and I also found them a potent aid in speech therapy. A Mobile Theatre had been started by a group of teachers to play to children, and in the secondary schools some of these brought puppets representing the three witches of 'Macbeth' or others designed for Kipling's story of 'How the Rhinoceros Got Its Skin'. Others again were made for dramatised versions of more familiar stories for the younger children. Classes in schools not only used the puppets but were motivated to make their own, some of which were quite excellent. I particularly remember the effect of translucent light in a Nativity play, in which shadow puppets had been inlaid with blue and red so that the light could shine through them. It was a sad loss indeed when many of Alice Taggart's stock, so exquisite in their workmanship, were found, in the course of one summer holiday, to have been destroyed by moths, which had somehow penetrated into the hamper in which they were stored.

At a later stage, when I was living with a friend named Isabel at Broughty Ferry and working in Dundee, I was again to find how excellent puppets were as an aid to speech training. My friend was a head lecturer in the methodology of teaching infants and even while I was in Aberdeen I had found her help quite invaluable. She was particularly good at using puppets and took special delight in performing plays and folksongs for the children, as well as encouraging them to make puppets for themselves.

On one occasion she had promised to take a puppet show out to one of the infant schools in Dundee and asked me to come and help. All the infants were sitting on the floor in front of the theatre and we came to one item in our programme which was the nursery rhyme, 'Hickory, dickory dock'. I was playing the mouse, manipulating the appropriate glove puppet on my right hand and holding on a concealed stick in my left a large clockface about seven inches in diameter. Isabel narrated the story while I made the 'mouse' run up the side of the clock to the figure one and down again. At that point she invited some members of our audience to come out and use a xylophone to make the sound of the clock striking one. Among several children who came forward, one little boy in particular proved outstandingly adept at striking the xylophone at exactly the right moment – just on the beat. So good was he at this that I felt I should congratulate him and, on enquiring his name of the teacher, discovered that it was Charlie. 'Oh Charlie,' I said, 'that was very good – well done, Charlie!' At this he turned round from his position at the side of the puppet theatre just below me on the left and asked, looking not at me but at the 'mouse' puppet I was holding, 'How do you know my name?' For a moment I was taken off my guard and couldn't think what answer to give him. Then, in a flash of inspiration I said: 'I am a magic mouse and know everyone's name.' The next second I realised what I might have let myself in for. All the children would begin asking the 'mouse' their names! Mercifully, at that moment Isabel drew the curtain. I was saved! Yet what remains indelibly fixed in my memory is that child's readiness to accept spontaneously and totally that the puppet I was manipulating was a real mouse who knew his name. As an example of how real puppets were to the children this is only one of many.

However, I digress. To return to those years I spent in Aberdeen, where my remit was to promote effective speech not only with younger children but with the older pupils as well. In those far-off days, of course, comprehensive education, either as an idea or as a reality, still lay in the distant future and the system of secondary education then in force was profoundly different. It was in 1945 that the division into two sectors, Junior and Senior Secondary, was introduced. Junior Secondary was considered appropriate to the so-called non-academic pupil, who would not be expected to continue on to higher education or to go to university. It was the pupils belonging to Senior Secondary who were deemed more suitable for such aims. The arguments as to the merits or demerits of such a system have been rehearsed over and over again both in speech and in writing, but for better or for worse, during my time in Aberdeen that was the system which prevailed.

Unless I had already taught them when they were younger, I found the Junior Secondary pupils far more difficult to work with than those in the Primary Sector. As a general rule, the measure of success which I was able to achieve with them depended largely on the quality of their English teacher. Indeed, my work was always regarded as connected with the

teaching of English. Certainly I met with much assistance and co-operation from those English teachers. Even though ignorant of drama in many
cases, they would be more than willing to enter into the dramatic aspects
and I would work these out for them. I might, for instance, orchestrate a
poem for choral speaking and, though many of the boys regarded poetry in
general as 'silly' and cissy', ballads, with their emphasis on energy and
heroism, would often be found acceptable. As a first step, therefore, it was
vital to find the right material.

A further activity in which I sometimes engaged with the pupils of the
Junior Secondary Sector was to put together a small dramatic programme
– it would last, perhaps, three quarters of an hour – which might include a
play and some ballads. Once we had mastered it, we would perform our
programme for the entertainment of the pupils at one or other of the
primary schools in the neighbourhood. Here too the willing co-operation
of a good English teacher of the Junior Secondary pupils was absolutely
vital. It was in connection with just such a programme, I believe, that I
first used the description, 'The Children's Theatre'. That was in one of my
early reports right back in 1943, when, of course, there was as yet neither
an organisation nor a building to which the title could be applied. It was
still necessary to give our programmes some name; otherwise we would
have found ourselves reduced to announcing them in some such words as:
'the boys and girls from class so-and-so in the Middle School (or from
Powis) will now entertain you.'

Of all the ways in which I managed to achieve the willing co-operation
of Junior Secondary pupils, that was one of my most successful. I must,
however reiterate: it depended totally for its success on the active support
of the English teachers. Another method was to make up collections of
speech games suitable for the various age groups. A typical instance
might be a game in which the participants had to work out descriptions of
things. In the Senior Secondaries one was always on easier ground, because they always had a Shakespeare play in the offing which would
provide suitable material for such games. Whatever form these exercises
might take, my consistent aim in all of them was to improve the pupils'
diction and even more articulation, which at this stage was more difficult.

Again, in my opening remarks I would deliberately adopt a slovenly
way of speaking and then ask: 'Now, what is wrong with the way in which
I am speaking to you?' They would point out that I was mumbling; that I
was failing to open my mouth so as to let the words out; that I was
probably not using my tongue sufficiently. They speedily became good at
analysing the problem. How far one could continue with such an approach

in order to motivate them depended on their mood. It was important always to assess the mood of a class and find the right material for them to work on, so that all of us could profit from speaking together.

It was vital from the outset to find a theme and collect as much material as possible, both prose and poetry, to illustrate it. The material could be used by either individuals or groups. The task of gathering it was in itself another way of capturing and retaining the pupils' interest. At the same time it supplied a framework within which to achieve my aims. I also found that I could stimulate and motivate them by recording their efforts on tape.

Every year we used to hold a Non-Competitive Festival which ran for a whole week. In this children from various schools put on performances of mime, choral verse, scenes from plays or puppetry for the entertainment of the rest. In 1962 we chose as that year's commentator a Mrs. Christabel Burniston, a very well-known lady who came from Southport. She was a specialist in 'oral English' and had established the English Speaking Board with its headquarters in Southport. She and her colleague, Miss Jocelyn Bell, would travel round the country examining groups of children in oral English. The examination itself took the form of a short talk on some subject of interest accompanied by appropriate visual aids. The speech would last about five minutes, though this depended on the stage which the pupil concerned had reached. The entrant then had to answer questions from the audience, which would consist of fellow participants. A selected passage of prose or a poem would also be prepared and spoken from memory, and the entrant would complete his or her task with a piece of unprepared sight reading.

The factors taken into account were the structure of the talk, the standard of speech, the use of the visual aids, the interpretation of the literature, the fluency of the reading and above all the relationship with the audience as evinced in the pupil's use of eye contact and response to questions. Though the atmosphere of these examinations was always made as pleasant and relaxed as possible, the assessment was quite rigorous.

We decided to invite secondary schools in Aberdeen to present pupils for this examination, on the understanding that I would be responsible for the necessary tuition and that it would take place either during or after school hours. Though we did not expect the response to our invitation to be overwhelming, we found in fact that within two days my timetable was full. The number of pupils, both boys and girls, whom I arranged to tutor came to no less than fifty-eight.

The challenge was tremendous and the work proved both highly interesting and lastingly beneficial. Certainly the preparation was time-consuming in the extreme. Finding the right material was difficult and sometimes entailed many hours of search before we could discover something that would appeal to the individual pupil. Many a young lad ended up by presenting Abraham Lincoln's Address to the Nation with its assertion that all men are created equal.

One particular class, from Frederick Street, sticks in my memory. The teacher said: 'We have sent you these children because they are very good generally at their other work, but are inclined to be hindered by their inability to speak.' That indeed was the case with so many. Though able pupils, they would be held back from expressing themselves orally by the fear of making fools of themselves.

As I have said, it was in 1962 that Christabel Burniston came to Aberdeen for the first ESB examination. It proved a tremendous success and some schools in Aberdeen are, I believe, still entering pupils. After it was over, Mrs. Burniston and I were sitting down over a cup of tea in King's Cafe in King Street when she said: 'Now, Catherine, what I want you to do is to send round a questionnaire for each of these boys and girls to answer anonymously.' Her aim was to obtain feedback on the Aberdeen pupils who had taken part and I duly sent out the questionnaire. One of the questions was, I remember: 'Do you have many opportunities to speak in the classroom situation?' In about nine out of ten cases the answer was somewhat on the following lines: 'We have two classes of oral English every week, but the teacher does most of the speaking herself'!

Oral English classes in those days consisted mainly in instructing the children in how to communicate rather than in spending the time on practical application. From then on, however, a marked shift of emphasis took place; 'learning by doing' became the keynote of such classes.

The ESB examinations I have described proved exactly what was needed for the secondary pupils who took part in them. Here they had a chance to express themselves in public and thereby to discover that they had the ability to do so. This in turn gave them the confidence to develop. A case in point arose many years later when I was selling my house in Broughty Ferry. The young man who came to survey it proved to be one of the chief surveyors of a Dundee firm, handsome and thoroughly businesslike. 'Don't you remember me?' he asked after he had looked into every corner of the house. 'I'm sorry but I'm afraid I don't,' I replied. 'I was in your oral English class in King Street', he said.

I was trained in 'elocution', which was concerned not so much with expressing one's own thoughts as with ways of effectively conveying someone else's. Now, as a result of this ESB experience in 1962, emphasis came to be laid on the successful communication of both one's own and other people's ideas and feelings.

All this may serve to illustrate how my work developed in both primary and secondary schools. As I look back on those years, I retain the warmest memories of the kindliness and encouragement I received from countless head teachers and class teachers, as well as from pupils and parents, in my efforts to help in developing the children's communication skills.

Chapter Seven

Festivals and Competitions

It will be clear that the new developments of which I have been speaking would have been impossible without the addition of more teachers to the Speech Training Department. The first speech training teacher was Miss Diane Greenhill, who was appointed in 1944. Thereafter the staffing gradually increased until, in 1955, an Assistant Chief Superintendent, a Mr. Ron Sawdon, was appointed. By the time I left in 1968, the staff had increased to sixteen full-time teachers of what was by then termed 'speech and drama'.

In 1945 a Poetry Festival was organised, in which children from various schools took part, and by 1952 this had become the Non-Competitive Festival of Poetry and Drama, Mime and Puppetry, which was held in the Children's Theatre in John Street. By 1954, the Festival ran for a week, with no less than twelve hundred children taking part. More of this, however, at a later stage.

We always had a guest commentator (never an adjudicator – the very nature of the Festival ruled that out), who at the end of the day would comment on the various performances. He or she would also send written comments to the pupils to help them with advice and encouragement.

In our efforts to encourage children to enter, we often had to overcome considerable diffidence on the part of the class teachers. 'Oh,' a teacher would say, 'I would like to take part but I don't know what to do.' Then I and my staff would set to to find them suitable material and to try it out with their pupils.

As for the children themselves, they loved this kind of work because they could see hundreds of other children performing. The Festival was not open to the public. Teachers would attend with their classes and gather ideas from what they saw which they could subsequently carry back and try out in their own schools.

One of the rules of the Festival was that in order to suggest the character he or she was portraying, each child could bring one and only one article of clothing with them and then only providing it was such as they could wear on public transport. They were also allowed one prop each, so long as it could be carried.

Our consistent aim was to promote an interest in language, both spoken and written, among children in the Primary and Secondary Sectors alike. To this end we also organised another activity in 1957, namely the Original Play and Poetry Writing Competition. Its purpose was to encourage pupils at different stages to write a play or poem, and they were allowed to choose any subject they liked. If their work, whether play or poem, was placed, members of the Children's Theatre would perform it in the Children's Theatre itself. After all, the fact that the child concerned had written the piece gave no grounds for assuming that he or she wished to be personally involved in performing it. In common with all playwrights, what they wanted was to see their work on the stage. After viewing the performance in the Children's Theatre, the winners came to receive their certificates there.

One incident concerning the writer of a poem which had won first prize remains vividly in my mind. She was a girl from King Street School and we invited her to come to a rehearsal of the poem and let us know whether our way of presenting it conformed to the way she herself had heard it in her head. She was also encouraged to put forward any other comments she felt inclined to make. That was exactly what she did and it turned out that on a number of points she disagreed with our interpretation. After due discussion of all aspects of the case, we finally arrived at a presentation which met with her desires. In this way both writer and performer were satisfied and all concerned were given the opportunity to be involved in creative collaboration.

Another memory of mine is of an especially lovely Nativity Play which had been written by a very young child. One particular scene, involving both Joseph and Mary, will remain for ever in my mind. It went as follows:

(Mary is sweeping the floor. Enter Joseph)
Joseph: I hear that Herod is going to kill all the boy babies.
Mary: Oh dear, if it's not one thing, it's another!
Joseph: I think we'd better leave. We'd better fly to Egypt.
Mary: All right, I'll do the packing. You get the donkey.
(Curtain. End of Scene.)

What could have been more effective than that?

Each year we used to invite an independent person to judge the competition. The judge I remember most vividly is the one who adjudicated this particular play. He was the late Mr. James Scotland, the Principal of Aberdeen College of Education. As a playwright himself, he appreciated the brevity and effectiveness of the scene I have quoted – so much so that he subsequently referred to it at several public dinners and other functions at which he was asked to speak.

After the Original Play and Poetry Writing Competition, our next venture was a Tape-Recording Competition which took place in 1961. By this time all schools were equipped with tape recorders, which constitute an excellent medium for the encouragement of clear, confident speech. All the schools were invited to compile their own programmes, which might include singing, choral speaking, interviews, speeches, poetry, documentaries etc.

So valuable did tape-recording prove as a medium that the headmistress of Kingswood Infant School, the late Isabel McHaffie, who was a brilliant headmistress, spent an afternoon with me inspecting the broadcasting system in use at Kingseat Hospital to broadcast messages throughout the building. I suggested to Isabel that she could install a similar system in her school. In encouraging her children to write, she was making use of a tape-recorder and they were taking a great interest in this approach. In short, almost all the necessary equipment was already at hand. The only item that appeared to be missing was a 'jack plug' for her tape-recorder. This was the start of the 'Kingswood Broadcasting Station', in which various announcers and interviewers took part, and the different classes performed for the benefit of everyone throughout the school. The vital importance of clear articulate speech in broadcasting was obvious to all concerned. They had to make themselves understood by everyone throughout the school.

I particularly remember one little girl being interviewed about a wedding which she had witnessed. Her own class teacher had been the bride, and she was beloved by all the children. The little girl was asked what her impressions had been on seeing her leave the church. I can still hear her voice as she replied, 'She was a b-e-a-u-t-i-f-u-l bride!'

Accustomed as they were to listening to the radio at home, the pupils now listened keenly to the way in which the 'broadcasters' presented their material, the more so since in those days not everyone had television in their homes. A further benefit from this activity was that they learned the social skills of politeness in the course of interviewing.

On occasions a pupil might select a Scottish poem in dialect to recite. 'Bawsy Broon' was one such and another example was chosen from William Souter's book, *Seeds in the Wind*. They also sang. Here, I realised, with children who could speak both Scots dialect and standard English, was an excellent opportunity to arouse their interest in the use of spoken language.

Apart from their work in schools and in the competitions and festivals I have described, the members of the speech training staff were also involved in work with the Mobile Theatre. On Wednesday afternoons programmes of mime, poetry, prose, puppetry and plays were arranged and rehearsed and then either taken on tour round the various schools or else performed in the Department itself for the benefit of visiting schools. Some of these programmes were designed for infants, others for secondary pupils. Our object in all this was to encourage children to take an interest in stories and read them for themselves. After the performances, the children were invited to write their comments, criticisms and suggestions and send them to me. The response, I found, was overwhelming.

Over the years, the Aberdeen Speech Training Department, which from 1954 onwards became the Speech and Drama Department, received innumerable visitors from overseas. It would be beyond me to record – let alone pronounce! – the names of all such visitors. We had educationalists, teachers and a whole range of people who were in some way or other involved and were interested in our methods of developing the ability of children to express themselves. Of all our activities, those which attracted far the greatest attention and which were to provide me personally with many of my happiest memories, were connected with the creation of the Aberdeen Children's Theatre.

Chapter Eight

The Aberdeen Children's Theatre

Although I had been trained in elocution and drama, I had at no time entertained any aspirations to become an actress. Nevertheless, as I went round the schools, I discovered that one of the most helpful ways of catching the interest and cooperation of the children was to introduce acting and movement into my teaching. It then struck me that though this was an art form which they unmistakably enjoyed, most of them had never been inside a theatre in their lives. The town did indeed boast a theatre, and a very beautiful one at that, but in 1942 it was very much a place for middle-class adults rather than children. I hasten to add that today this is far from being the case; many delightful productions suitable for children are included in its present-day programmes.

As early as 1945, therefore, a group of young and enthusiastic class teachers in the city set up, under my leadership, a teachers' dramatic society called The Motley Players. They toured the area performing programmes similar to those which we had formerly presented with The Summer Players, as well as putting on one-act plays at the local Aberdeen Festivals. For the benefit of senior pupils in the secondary schools, they also tackled such plays as Chekhov's 'Cherry Orchard', James's 'The Heiress' or Goldsmith's 'She Stoops to Conquer'.

A subdivision of The Motley Players came to be known as The Children's Theatre. On Saturday mornings they used to perform, for the primary Schools' children's benefit, plays which they had rehearsed during the week. In those days the title 'Children's Theatre', which I had invented, was applied both to this subdivision of The Motley Players and, as I mentioned earlier, to performances which secondary pupils used to put on for the primary school children. In those days, however, no actual building existed to which the name 'Children's Theatre' could be at-

57

tached, nor had it yet come to be reserved for the new enterprise which was to develop, that namely of children performing with children. I must now relate how the Children's Theatre as an activity was started and how a building came to be acquired for it and called by its name. I was convinced that we needed both.

As early as 1947, in my annual report to the Town Council's Education Committee, I put forward the suggestion that 'It would be a great help if the Committee would keep in mind the need for a little theatre with an auditorium similar to the Students' Union – and centrally situated – which would be available as a "Children's Theatre" and as a "Theatre of Youth", the age groups being respectively eight to twelve and twelve to seventeen.'

By 1949 accommodation had been made available on Saturday mornings in the form of the dining hall (or dining hut, as it should perhaps be called) of the Technical College in John Street. A stage was built for us, complete with curtain, and the windows were also curtained. Our 'goings on' were the subject of constant criticism on the part of the janitor and in consequence of this we also had a cupboard built in one corner of the hall in which our equipment could be housed. Before we started work all chairs and tables had to be cleared out of the way, and at the end they had to be replaced. Though in that year of 1949 conditions were far from ideal, we did make a start, for the teachers who had formed the subdivision of The Motley Players, and who were still thought of as members of The Children's Theatre, put on Hans Anderson's 'The Tinder Box' and 'Rumpelstiltskin'. In that little theatre they gave eight performances for the children during school hours.

By 1951 plays were included as part of the Festival of Britain celebrations. By this time children were proposing votes of thanks and acting as chairpersons. In that year too, students from the senior class of the Pre-Nursing College gave Children's Theatre performances of 'Hansel and Gretel'.

Still the John Street accommodation was causing us difficulties. After the annual Festival of Poetry, Drama, Mime and Puppetry in June, 1952, I wrote to the Education Committee complaining bitterly of the unsatisfactory conditions we had had to endure. While we were working, classes had been taking place upstairs, and the Festival had been constantly interrupted by boys of the Technical College moving around. What they must have felt about our performances is anyone's guess, but all I was concerned with was the Festival itself! In my report for that year to the Education Committee, therefore, I expressed the following heartfelt plea for a headquarters of our own:-

The Children's Theatre production of 'Rumplestiltskin', played by children to children, 1956.

'At present all administration, conferences, filing, interviews with teachers, parents and children, writing of reports and other such matters have to be undertaken in one small room with a clerical assistant also present. Heating and ventilation are entirely unsatisfactory. The room is approximately fourteen by ten feet and eight feet three inches high, with one small window eighteen inches by nineteen inches as the only source of fresh air.

'The Children's Theatre in John Street has filled an immediate need but, as I have said, it is no longer big enough and it is quite unsuitable for rehearsals owing to noise and interruptions.'

While John Street was beset by all these difficulties, children from various schools were performing programmes in the Aberdeen Art Gallery at lunchtimes consisting of verse speaking, mime and puppetry or alternatively of excerpts from scripted plays. One such school was the one nowadays called Gilcomstoun School, though in those days it was known as Skene Street. I had been working with a 'primary six' class there, whose teacher, a Miss Edwards, was particularly interested in what I was trying to do. She was most eager for her children to be able to communicate well and was keen on the reciting of choral verse in her class. As I had a large stock of material from which to choose suitable poems for her children, we worked together especially well. It came as no surprise, therefore, that when it was her class's turn to perform a programme of choral verse in the Art Gallery it was an outstanding success. The audience unmistakably enjoyed it and so did we; but – far more importantly – so did the children themselves!

Having worked with this particular class for some weeks, the thought came to me: 'These children are not performing as well as this just because they have been asked to; they are actually doing it with relish. I wonder how this interest and enthusiasm can be encouraged to develop.' It was then that I thought of inviting them to come to John Street on a Saturday morning and indulge their interest further. I suggested that we form a little group and make an attempt at performing folk songs or plays of some kind, eventually, perhaps, putting together a programme of such material.

Through the Director's weekly Letter to the schools, other children came to hear of our new enterprise and asked to join. Soon our little group had grown to twenty. This degree of interest surprised me; I had never intended developing our small initiative into a major event. Nevertheless, the members of our little group proved willing workers, never missing a single morning. So interested were they, in fact, that there was never any need for disciplinary measures. After working together for some time, we actually put on a little performance.

From such small beginnings then and initially from a handful of the children of Skene Street School, membership of the Children's Theatre grew and grew. Before long the Town Council had come to appreciate the fact that we needed a place of our own. Clearing the stage each week was a hard business; so too was the task of storing all our equipment in one small cupboard. Thus the search for a building began. It all took time, however, so that it was not until 1955 that we were offered the little hall of what was then the North Church in King Street. I well remember the experience of viewing the premises with an inspector sent by the Scottish Education Department. Though small and inconvenient, the building did fulfil our supreme and overriding requirement, namely to have a place of our own. No more putting away of chairs or trying to stuff all our possessions into a single small cupboard! Thenceforward I had a permanent place in which to hold my classes in oral English. Even more, it was destined to become the Children's Theatre and, much later on, the theatre of The Longacre Players.

In the course of 1956, while the building was being altered, I made my first visit abroad. I had somewhere read that a Children's Theatre movement was active in Stockholm and I arranged with the Scottish Education Department that I should go and see what was being done there. So far as I was concerned, however, it proved a great disappointment. While I enjoyed my visit to Stockholm, I could learn nothing new about Children's Theatre. The Swedish version seemed to amount to nothing more than an activity aimed at keeping children off the streets. There was neither literary nor social emphasis, nor was there any consistency of membership. From the children's point of view, it was simply a way of passing an evening. The one point that did impress me, however, was the range and quality of the facilities which had been provided in Stockholm, notably the little theatre and its seating capacity, which consisted of tip-up chairs for one hundred and eighty. Workshops for the making of clothes and scenery, and even cloakrooms for the audience, had also been provided.

My next visit was to America. It was arranged and organised in association with the North Western University at Evanstone, Illinois. Here I found myself greatly impressed by the woman running the Children's Theatre, whose name was Winifred Ward. Even there, however, I failed to learn anything really new. Certainly Winifred Ward had all the right ideas, but Children's Theatre as practised there was confined to a careful selection of middle-class boys and girls, and again the emphasis was purely on acting. What was missing, once more, was the social factor. In the Children's Theatre in Aberdeen, by contrast, children were never excluded, whatever their background or the school they came from. All that was required was that they were keen and accepted the discipline – which they did.

The next time I was invited to visit a Children's Theatre abroad I was highly honoured for I went as a member of a British Theatre Delegation to Russia. The delegation included a lecturer in Russian from one of the English universities, an architect interested in theatre architecture, and that brilliant ballet dancer and director, Marie Rambert. The reason I was included to represent the Children's Theatre movement was probably that I was the only one involved in such work in Britain at that time. Tremendous as the experience was in many ways, and impressed as I felt at what I saw of the Russians' Children's Theatre, I was forced to conclude once more that their theatre was nothing like ours; what they meant by Children's Theatre was adult professional actors acting for the benefit of children.

So far as I could discover, therefore, while Children's Theatre movements did exist in various parts of the world, nothing was to be found quite like that which we had envisaged for Aberdeen.

31 King Street – how vividly it still stands in my memory! Downstairs it had a workshop and make-up rooms. On the ground floor was the theatre itself, complete with a little stage and about a hundred tip-up seats. On the first floor was a large room suitable for movement and fencing or for rehearsals. We christened it the Lecture Room. On that floor too were the lavatories and cloakrooms. At the very top were the attics, in which there was room for a caretaker's flat and my office. In passing, it is interesting to note that throughout my life my offices have consistently been on the roof, in attics or else next to public lavatories! However, that never bothered me in the slightest. I always appeared to be operating on a shoestring, but what mattered, I believed, was the imagination, the vitality, the creativity that could be engendered.

Hence it was that in May, 1958 The Children's Theatre in King Street was opened by the actress Flora Robson. The children presented a programme of original plays by boys and girls between the ages of ten and sixteen. For the occasion the theatre was gaily decorated with most attractive murals, which had been painted by members of St. Peter's R.C. School. In my annual report I wrote as follows:

'Since transferring this activity to our own premises at 31 King Street, there has been a continual expansion of this work. Although the building

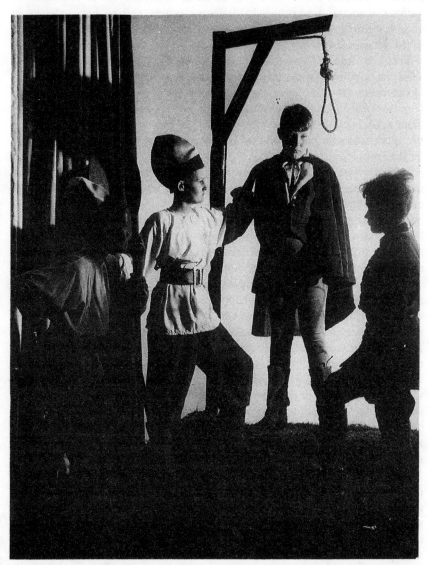

The Children's Theatre production of 'The Tinderbox' by Nicholas Stuart Gray in the Aberdeen Children's Theatre, King Street, December 1958. Malcolm Rennie standing by the scaffold.

is small (the auditorium holds only one hundred and ten children), and the demand for tickets can never be satisfied, it is possible to organise the various associated activities in different rooms and so have classes in speech training, improvisation, make-up, mime and movement in addition to the rehearsals proper.'

This Children's Theatre in Aberdeen was the only municipal one of its kind. The children of the city have much for which to thank the Education Committees of that time, together with Mr. Frank Scorgie, who was Director of Education when the decision was made to find a building, and most especially to Mr. J.R. Clark, who had become Director by the time the work was completed and who took so much interest in all that happened there.

A fact of which we could never lose sight was that, for all the work involved, the Children's Theatre was just another experiment. I am not sure whether it would ever have got off the ground at all had it not been for the untiring help given by my friend Isabel McHaffie, who was later to become head teacher of Kingswood Infant School in Aberdeen, and later still Head of Infant Education at Dundee College of Education. She stood by me in all the difficulties which had to be overcome before the project actually took off, and once it did she did so much to engender an atmosphere of trust and happiness. In fact the enthusiasm with which she threw herself into the whole project was no less than my own; when she was not applying make-up she would be playing the piano. The children were deeply attached to her and I myself owe her a great debt.

Another important group of people to whom I owe a debt of gratitude was to be met with in the Aberdeen Corporation Workshop. They always made me feel like an honorary member and when I needed a prop or piece of scenery, they never failed to do their utmost to help me. So welcoming and so willing an attitude did they invariably show, that I always felt myself among friends.

Another piece in the jigsaw of human helpers and a highly important one at that was Mrs. Farquhar, the caretaker at 31 King Street, who lived in the flat next door to my attic office. She was kindness itself and we shared a mutual respect for the building. She loved to see a clean little theatre with all its seats welcoming and everything in its place. After the shows she used to say: 'I aye ken fine when it's a children's audience. The place is that much cleaner. They dinna throw things about!' Many and many were the times when, having no time for a meal, I was kept going by her cups of coffee. I shall always be grateful to her.

A further development of the Children's Theatre was embarked upon in 1958. A new housing scheme had been established at Mastrick and a new Community Centre had been set up with Mr. Gordon Rennie as warden. It was arranged that every Saturday morning two teachers would go there and try to encourage a branch of the Children's Theatre in the area. A parent committee was formed to help with costumes and props, and the members of this enjoyed the honour of a visit by the wife of Sir Donald Wolfit.

As I have pointed out, The Children's Theatre attracted many visitors and they always seemed to be struck by one point in particular: the behaviour of the children. This was particularly true of breaktimes, while they were having their lemonade. Visitors supposed that this would be a time of mayhem, which was far from being the case. The children had no need to find extra uses for their energy because it was fully engaged in the various activities taking place both before and after breaktime. They were encouraged to be courteous to visitors, who for their part took great pleasure in moving about among the children and in speaking to them.

As I was to write in another of my reports concerning our Children's Theatre:

'Membership represents an interesting cross-section of society. This is indeed a "comprehensive body" and care is taken to maintain standards of courtesy and behaviour which would be acceptable to all parents.'

I cannot sufficiently emphasise the social aspect of the project. So far as I was concerned, what the children's backgrounds were did not matter. All I knew for certain was that these were the adults of the future, who were destined to mix with all levels of society. I wanted them to be able to do so with confidence. What may have made this doubly important to me, I believe, were memories of my own feelings of insecurity during childhood and adolescence. In my case, however, I was too good an actress to let such feelings show. These children, I felt, had to achieve something far more radical than a mere capacity to cover up their feelings. I wanted them to have a confidence that was genuine and that would flow from their ability to communicate easily and fluently through speech. There was a further attitude which I was anxious to inculcate in them: to show the same respect and enthusiasm towards me that I showed in my dealings with them. I wanted them to learn good manners as well as consideration for others and a readiness to help them. In my 1963 Report I wrote:

'Much misunderstanding exists of Children's Theatre work and it is necessary to emphasise that it is not intended to train actors and actresses or to encourage precocious children. It might be more accurate to describe the activities which take place in King Street and Mastrick Community Centre on Saturday mornings as 'Classes in creative activities associated with drama', since much emphasis is laid upon improvisation, mime and movement, fencing and scene painting and make-up in addition to the formalities of rehearsing a scripted play. One can observe an increase in self-confidence, greater awareness and imaginative power and a happy relationship between staff and children which leads to a natural courtesy.'

The numbers of children involved in the Children's Theatre were by now increasing so rapidly that more space was needed. Accordingly, in 1967, the Education Committee made the Aberdeen Arts Centre available for our use on Saturday mornings. The building lay just next door to the Children's Theatre and in my annual report for that year I reminded the Committee of the importance of these extra premises.

'Accommodation is a greater problem than staffing and without the use of the rooms and the stage in the Arts Centre, when available, this project would break down.'

In fact the Education Committee of that time took great pride in their Aberdeen Children's Theatre and gave us every help and support. After all, it was the first municipal Children's Theatre of its kind in this country. For their consistently helpful attitude I am extremely grateful.

Since those times The Children's Theatre has gone from strength to strength. Today it is still flourishing as a result of the excellent work of a team of speech and drama teachers led by Margaret Hearne. Margaret in particular, I know, has brought unstinting effort and tireless dedication to the work she has done for young people over the years. I am only sorry that by the time she joined the Department I had already left; hence I never had the opportunity of working with her. Under her aegis the Children's Theatre has mounted many impressive productions and at the same time encouraged new writing by commissioning several plays to be performed. While the present team of teachers still endeavours to achieve the highest standards of performance, they still uphold those principles of awareness of and respect for others which I laid down all those years ago. Over eighty children attend, from a whole range of schools throughout the area, still representing a social cross-section of the community. The Children's Theatre is nowadays run by the Education Department of Grampian Region.

It gives me particular pleasure to report all this, for I regard the Aberdeen Children's Theatre as one of my most successful projects and one of which I am immensely proud. It provides true bridges of communication, but like all bridges, if they are to be effective, once built they have to be maintained. In the arrangements that have been made for the bridge that is the Children's Theatre, despite all the efforts of the teachers working in it, one flaw is to be found. The weekly use of the Arts Centre is no longer granted; the time which used to be made available has been devoted to other purposes. It is true that, contrary to my prediction in 1967, the project has not actually broken down in consequence but the fact remains that the ensuing lack of space causes considerable difficulties. On Saturday mornings the children have to be moved between two different sites, The Children's Theatre building in King's Street and the Aberdeen University Debater in Marischal College.

Though I am no longer in a position to do anything personally, I strongly believe that a new building should be provided for the young people involved, equipped with stage, auditorium, practice rooms and canteen, and that the person in charge of the organisation should also have complete charge of the building itself.

Let us return, however, to the sixties. As publicity for the Children's Theatre grew, so did the number of visitors to it. In 1966 the BBC actually made a film about it called 'Bridges to Cross'. Before long television companies were seeking children to appear in various of their productions. Children took part in such series as 'This Man Craig', 'The Borderers' and 'Dr. Finlay's Casebook'. In connection with Dr. Finlay, it is interesting to notice that though all the principal actors of the original version are now dead, a new series is being made with a new cast and that the title role is being played by one of the old members of The Longacre Players. Who, then, are these Longacre Players? That story must be told in another chapter.

Chapter Nine

The Longacre Players

Late one afternoon in 1963 I had just entered my office when one of my typists informed me that even though it was after school hours, a deputation was waiting to see me in the lecture room. 'Who are they?' I enquired. 'Some of the older members of the Children's Theatre,' she replied. Sure enough, I found seven or eight young people waiting for me. Though I cannot now remember all their names, those of Malcolm Rennie, Dorothy Foote and Alan Cowie do stick in my mind. They began by pointing out that since they had reached the age of sixteen, they had become too old for the Children's Theatre and according to the rules I had had to bid them farewell. Space had to be made for younger children to join. They went on to explain that they had been discussing this sad state of affairs among themselves, and the outcome of their deliberations was that they had come to ask whether I would be prepared to organise a senior group for them.

Though the suggestion had taken me by surprise, my reply was immediate. 'Yes' I will do this for you but I'll make my own conditions. The first is that you will, as a group, enter the Scottish Community Drama Association Festival. You must understand that if you agree to do so, you will have to be prepared to learn a lot of technique that so far has not been necessary.' As I have already explained, the Children's Theatre was not concerned with the training of actors and actresses. The Community Drama Festival was a different matter. The proposed group would be subjected to criticism by a professional adjudicator, which meant that the members would have to learn about stage techniques in all their aspects.

'Up to now,' I continued, 'you have had highly complimentary things said about you both by your grannies, aunties etc. and by the papers. From now on it will be very different. I need your promise that you will attend rehearsals and work as hard as I ask you to. I am prepared to do my bit, but I do need your promise. Go away and think about it now, because it will mean rehearsals every Friday, and probably on Sunday afternoons as well. Your Sunday lunch will have to be sandwiches and flasks of coffee, with which you will have to arm yourselves beforehand. Think carefully before you commit yourselves!'

The upshot was as I expected. After due and careful consideration they agreed to all my conditions. For them this was a considerable step; from now onwards they would have to make a thorough study of stage technique.

During that first year the play we chose to perform for the S.C.D.A. Festival was 'Count Albany'. It was a good one-act play and we worked at it very hard. The members of the new group never missed a single rehearsal either on Friday evenings or on Sunday afternoons, which we used for additional rehearsals as the date of the Festival drew near. We brought our coffee and sandwiches and ate them on the roof of the Children's Theatre, overlooking the skyline of Aberdeen. This, for some reason unknown to me, caused immense delight. It would have been in January or February that our additional Sunday rehearsals would have taken place, for it was always about that time that the Festival itself was held. Many a Sunday afternoon did we spend huddled in scarves, overcoats and gloves to brave the weather of the north-east.

That particular Festival was held in the High School for Girls, because the disused church which afterwards became the Arts Centre had not yet been put to this use. Before it opened, we had to choose a name for our group. Since these were older children, I was unwilling to enter them as belonging to the Children's Theatre. Now someone who had given persistent and significant support to all the work that we undertook both in speech and drama was Mr. J.R. Clark, the Director of Education. In seeking a name for the group, therefore, it was to him that I turned for inspiration. Once again he did not fail me. 'Well,' he said, 'What about Longacre? There used to be a monastery of that name in this part of Aberdeen – why not The Longacre Players?'

After the Council had granted our new group permission to use the name, we duly entered for the Festival as 'The Longacre Players'. On the night of the Festival itself, despite being, of course, a completely unknown quantity, we actually found that we had been placed first! As always at these festivals, the public adjudication was followed by a private one. I remember being made a little late for this; so many people kept stopping me to ask who these Longacre Players were! When at last I

The Motley Players in a production of 'Happy Journey' by Thornton Wilder, 1959.

opened the door of the room in which the private adjudication was being
held, it was to find the team sitting there, clean and tidy in their school
blazers. Yet nothing appeared to be happening. 'The team has not arrived
yet,' the adjudicator said to me. 'There they are,' I replied, 'sitting in the
front row!' 'Oh,' he said in surprise, 'but those are only schoolchildren!'
'So they are, but they are the ones who have just acted "Count Albany".'

For those youngsters to have succeeded so well at their very first
attempt was, of course, a tremendous thrill. Furthermore, it placed The
Longacre Players firmly on the map in the field of amateur drama.

When the group was first formed, a second condition for membership
had been generally recognised and accepted, though in this case it had
hardly needed to be explicitly laid down. Only those who had previously
belonged to the Children's Theatre and had grown too old for it would be
eligible to join. This, I felt, would ensure that every member would
already be thoroughly familiar with the system under which I operated.
They would know that each member would have to do his or her share in
the workshop and be ready to perform odd jobs, sometimes having very
little of the actual acting falling to their lot. In general they would have to
know and abide by the rules pertaining to responsible and socially acceptable behaviour. If they had met my standards in these respects in the
Children's Theatre, their reward was to be promoted to the senior group
when they reached the required age. In practice, this rule was not rigidly
adhered to and exceptions were made; nevertheless, it did ensure that the
spirit and values of the Children's Theatre lived on undiminished in the
Longacre Players.

As a group they were, on any showing, outstandingly dedicated and
hardworking, keen to learn technique and practise the craft of the actor. In
1968, when the time came for me to retire from my work as Superintendent of the City Speech and Drama Department and to say goodbye to all
those with whom I had worked, I took my leave of them happy in the
knowledge that they had acquired a valuable grounding in the techniques
of acting. I was confident that they were in a position, if they so chose, to
embark upon a career in the professional theatre. Even if they remained
amateurs, they would be outstandingly good ones. Either way, I knew that
they would be able to give and to receive great pleasure from their work in
the field of theatre.

As it turned out, quite a number of those original members of The
Longacre Players did choose to make careers for themselves in theatre
or television. Malcolm Rennie became an actor in London's West End
and also on television. Alan Cowie became an editor with Grampian

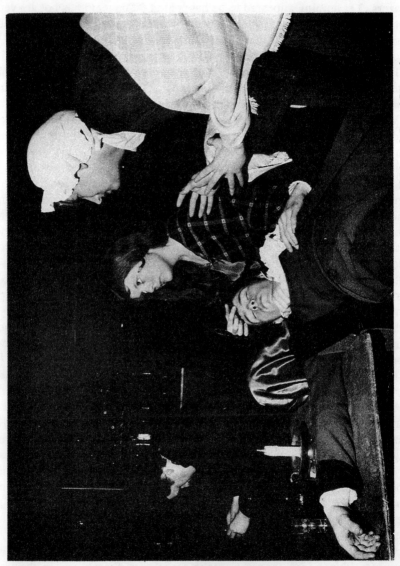

The Longacre Players' production of 'The Anatomist' by James Bridie, 1966, with David Rintoul.

Television. John Duffus became an impresario and is currently involved in operatic management. Several others, notably Dorothy Foote, Jennifer Smith and Irene Valentine became speech and drama teachers in schools. One member of The Longacre Players who had not first gone through the ranks of the Children's Theatre was a certain David Wilson, who subsequently became known as David Rintoul. He also became a professional actor and is currently appearing on television as the new 'Dr. Finlay'. He had already auditioned for a part in the original series, but had been considered at the time to be too young for it.

For me, both The Children's Theatre and The Longacre Players hold the fondest of memories. The same is true, I know, of many who were involved in their work whether as members or as teachers. Parents too were generous in their appreciation of what was achieved for their children. Many were the letters we received expressing this attitude, and one in particular may be regarded as typical:

'I cannot sufficiently express my thanks to you [those working with the children] for what you have done to develop the confidence of my son. He would never have taken his place in school and society as he does now so happily, if it had not been for his association with The Children's Theatre.'

Since those far-off days in 1941, when I had been appointed as the sole teacher of speech, I had explored many avenues, accepted many challenges and worked in collaboration with an ever-increasing staff. From the account I have given it will be apparent that, in terms of time, my job was far from being confined to weekdays or to the hours of nine to five. I worked a seven-day week with many evenings thrown in. If I had rendered an account for all the hours I had worked, the total bill would have been astronomical. At the same time it must be remembered that it was not only speech and drama work that fell within my remit. I was also responsible for all the speech therapy work carried out in Aberdeen.

Chapter Ten

Speech Therapy in Aberdeen

My work in speech therapy in Aberdeen followed a course which was separate from, though parallel to, that of my work in speech and drama. In order to trace it I must at this point return to the year 1941, when I was first appointed 'speech teacher'. As I have previously explained, exactly what areas of work were intended to be included under this umbrella term was anyone's guess! Until I had gone round the schools, I did not know myself what my work would involve. When I did discover this I realised, to my dismay, that it had nothing to do with 'elocution'. What it did have to do with was how people spoke, how they made words, how they shaped them and which organs they used. Accordingly, my approach to my new task was along these lines.

Aware as the teachers were that speech was my specialised field, it was natural that they should have brought to my notice those children in their classes who stammered or evinced some other difficulty – a lisp, for instance, or a cleft palate, which in those days was not uncommon. My training in speech therapy had familiarised me with certain techniques which could be used to help children suffering from impediments of this kind. Nevertheless, I always had to explain to the teachers that I had not been appointed as a therapist. It soon became abundantly clear that in those days most people failed to appreciate the fine distinction between speech training and speech therapy. Despite having some factors in common, the aims and procedures in each case were entirely different. Speech training was concerned with the improvement of normal speech (or at least what appeared to be such); speech therapy aimed at the rehabilitation of a faculty which had broken down.

Again I have already pointed out that at that stage in my career my real interest lay in speech therapy. I was aware, moreover, that though it was

74

not the role assigned to me, a need did exist for a speech therapist in Aberdeen. It did not take too long for the members of the Education Committee to realise that fact for themselves and to appoint a speech therapist. Until that appointment was made, however, I worked in the evening clinic at Woolmanhill Hospital on a voluntary basis.

Of the various patients whom I treated, I remember in particular a young woman of perhaps twenty or so who used to come to me at the clinic at the end of her working day. Whether she worked in a fish factory or as a typist I cannot now remember, but in any case she suffered from a very bad stammer. After devoting much thought to her case and to the question of how best to help her, I decided that I would practise a particular kind of stammer myself and then try it out in a shop with her beside me.

The first place in which I put my experiment to the test was the lounge of the Gloucester Hotel. It served as a meeting-point for the speech therapy peer group, which used to have coffee there. That particular morning I happened to arrive first and as the waiter approached I was thinking what kind of stammer to use in addressing him: was it to be a repetitive one or one in which the sufferer opens his mouth and then finds it impossible to proceed at all? As I was ordering my cup of coffee I deliberately stammered badly on the 'c', with an expression full of strain and tension on my face. 'What's the matter with you?' was the waiter's reaction, 'You were all right yesterday!' On looking up I discovered that it was the head waiter himself, who was an old friend of mine. He must have thought me decidedly odd! This, however, did not deter me, when the girl came to the clinic, from arranging to accompany her on a shopping expedition that same night. When I suggested the experiment her face fell. 'I will do the shopping,' I reassured her, 'All you have to do is to watch whether there is anything different about how I am acting; if you notice anything, tell me afterwards what it is. You won't have to do anything at all beyond that.'

At that time a little general grocery shop stood on the corner of the road off Skene Square, just a few yards away from Woolmanhill Hospital. That evening, accompanied by my patient, I walked into the shop, approached the counter and, showing terrible strain in my lips, asked for 'a b-b-box of m-m-matches'. 'Oh, what a nuisance that must be to you,' said the man who was serving me. 'It is, it is!' I replied, 'But thankyou for your k-k-kindness.'

As we left the girl remarked: 'One thing I would not have done was to look at the man when I spoke to him.'

'Well,' I replied, 'the next time you meet someone you know, keep your eyes on them while you are speaking to them and tell them what you are doing.' This was the way in which together we made one step forward in learning how to cope with her stammer. The technique of eye-contact did in fact help her confidence.

· Another of my venues was the Sick Children's Hospital, where I used to go on Saturday mornings until my work there had to yield pride of place to that of the Children's Theatre. The children treated there came from an area far wider than the city of Aberdeen itself and they included many stammerers. Others suffered from cleft palate operations which had turned out to be only partially successful. They were left with a nasal quality in their speech of which they could be acutely conscious. Such cases would be referred to me by the doctor concerned.

My position, then, was somewhat extraordinary: whereas in my chosen field of speech therapy I was now practising on a voluntary basis, what I was actually being paid for was my work in speech training!

In those far-off days the Hospital authorities had not assessed the need for a speech therapist. All that was required, they believed, was for me to attend on certain days each week and take eight or ten patients who lived in the Aberdeen area. By 1943, however, they had come to recognise the need and in that year they appointed a Miss Kay McAllister as full-time speech therapist. In the early stages four different districts had clinics set up in them, which were attended by children of nine years or older. Those younger than nine were visited by Miss McAllister or myself.

In 1944 I made a plea for more help with the under-nines for, as I said in my report for that year, 'This is a good time for treatment, and much may be done before the habit factor has become too strongly fixed and the consciousness of a speech defect has produced its inevitable emotional reactions.'

In the following year the entire work-load was still being coped with by only one therapist and myself. In my 1945 Report I made a plea for others to be appointed:

'It is generally recognised that the proportion of therapists in Britain is one to ten thousand of the school population, assuming three hundred speech defects. In Aberdeen there is only one for the entire city with a total population of twenty-four thousand.'

In 1947 another therapist was appointed and before long others were being added until, in 1953, our total strength amounted to six therapists manning six clinics. They came from all over Scotland and England; word had spread that at least in Aberdeen prospective speech therapists stood a good chance of finding work. Once appointed, they would have a good clinic with their own telephone. Such pieces of equipment as tape recorders, blackboards and books – anything, in fact, that would be of help to the children – would be supplied, as well as trolleys on which to move them about. From the first I had insisted that the therapists had decent clinics in which to work and Aberdeen provided them, purpose-built in many cases, with all the equipment that would be needed either for pre-school children brought in by their mothers, or for school children living in the area concerned. Each district had its own clinic, complete with every mechanical aid that could be desired.

In addition to the work the therapists did for the children, we also organised meetings for the mothers of stammerers. We believed that in cases of stammering it was vital for all who came in contact with the sufferer to understand the problem and operate on the same basis as the therapist. Instances had arisen of either teachers or parents falling victim to the common belief that stammering was a purely physical defect and so giving advice to the child that contradicted the therapist's approach. They were trying to deal with the effect without understanding the cause.

While I would very much have liked to take part in the speech therapy work, I had so many commitments in speech and drama that it became impracticable for me to do so. Speech therapists, having all been trained on the same lines and passed the same examinations, were in this sense better prepared in their field. They could be relied upon from the outset to get on with their work by themselves and with a large measure of independence. By contrast, the work being undertaken in speech training and drama was at that time new and exploratory and, as a result, I found myself having to spend a great deal of time with the teachers. Even so, if a therapist fell ill or had to be absent for any reason, I would stand in for her. As an aid to my work in speech therapy, I would sometimes employ drama techniques. In Skene Square, I remember, we had a puppet theatre and I had some glove puppets of my own which I used with a group of little boys. One of these had a bad stammer, yet when I put the children behind the curtain with puppets on their hands, I found to my surprise that the one with the stammer was not stammering at all. He was concentrating on speaking as the puppet and was engrossed in the task to the exclusion of all else.

This same boy used to come to the Children's Theatre. We were putting on a play about 'Fat King Melon', in the course of which an old woman had to cross the stage with her little grandson, speaking to him all the way. When I asked the little boy with the stammer to take the part of the

At the Aberdeen Children's Theatre.

grandson, a new problem arose: he would not stop speaking! Once in the role of another person, he was both confident and fluent. In certain cases this proved a new and interesting approach to the problems of speech therapy, though it always depended on the individual concerned. Some reacted well while with others the technique seemed to make no difference.

Nevertheless I became deeply interested in the use of puppetry as a therapeutic aid. By 1945 it had been amply proved how valuable puppets could be. When speaking for their puppets behind a curtain, younger children would often lose their fear and shyness. As a result, a stock of puppets was procured for the Speech Therapy Department. Nor was I slow to point out the value of puppetry in speech therapy. In my 1947 Report to the Education Committee I wrote:

'Therapeutic puppetry has been used with great benefit for maladjusted and neurotic children by Dr. Simone Marcus in Paris. This method of psychiatry has also been tried with much success in the Children's Ward at the Bellevue Hospital in New York.'

Working with children in the early 1960s.

During my time in Aberdeen I did little work with adults. The reason was that even though my staff worked in the Hospital, much of the more difficult work which they undertook was such as I would never have counted myself able to do. I knew enough about speech therapy to realise that it was a young and developing profession and that any one of the girls who had passed examinations in it had studied branches of the subject which were unfamiliar to me. In consequence, in the field of speech therapy I felt far happier working with schoolchildren.

Although I organised the speech therapy work and had to write the annual reports for that Department too, I spent less time on that branch than on speech training and drama. Yet speech therapy was precisely the field in which I had always been most interested. My time was to come!

In 1968 I retired from my post as Superintendent of Speech and Drama and Speech Therapy in Aberdeen and returned south once more, this time to Dundee. By this time I was sixty-four but I was far from ready to stop working and began looking round for something to do. Certainly Dundee seemed uninterested in any Children's Theatre work, but when the Education Committee there offered me a job in speech therapy I took it, expecting to find conditions of work similar to those which I had come to know in Aberdeen. I soon found how different Dundee was!

Chapter Eleven

Work with Stroke Patients in Dundee

Even before I arrived in Dundee, I received a letter from the neurologist at the Royal Infirmary there. He had been informed of my coming and was inviting me to join his staff in the Neurological Department as Speech Therapist. Though I recognised that I had been most highly honoured, I felt at the same time that this was the one aspect of my profession for which I was altogether unprepared. I therefore wrote back expressing my appreciation but explaining that I was woefully lacking in up-to-date knowledge of the subject. If only I had known then the path along which I was so soon to be led!

Once arrived in the city, I found that as far as dramatic work was concerned, little or no interest existed. Certainly the Dundee College of Education seemed quite indifferent to work in the realm of Children's Theatre. Accordingly, when the Education Committee offered me a job as speech therapist in the schools, I had no hesitation in accepting. It was then that I found how far below the excellent working conditions made available in Aberdeen were those prevailing in Dundee. To give one instance, I remember occasions on which no room whatever could be found for me in the particular school I was visiting, so that I was forced to take the children I was treating in the back of my car.

In another case, I recall a teacher saying to me: 'This little girl does not speak. I wonder whether you would take her and tell me what to do with her?' 'Where can we go?' I asked. 'Well,' she replied, 'the only place I can think of is the sewing cupboard. There simply isn't anywhere else.' That, therefore, is where the small girl and I had to conduct our interview. It turned out to be a typical sewing room cupboard, piled from top to bottom with boxes and materials. Those who have experience of such things will be able to appreciate the amount of space available – or rather

81

the lack of it! On opening the door, I had to stand back to let the small girl in. 'There aren't any chairs,' I explained as I shut it behind her, 'so you have that box to sit on and I'll take this one.' The moment I sat down on the box I had selected it collapsed beneath me. We both shrieked with laughter and from that moment onwards she never stopped speaking! When I saw her teacher again after our session I hardly knew what to say. 'Well,' I reported, 'I don't know what's wrong with her under normal conditions, but all the time she has spent with me in that little cupboard she has been speaking continuously!'

Working conditions generally, however, were so bad that eventually I decided to give up the job in the schools. It had afforded me no opportunities to exercise my skills in therapy, and in any case a chance now arose of working in the hospital.

Here again I found that conditions were in sad contrast to those of Aberdeen. For all that, the accommodation, though primitive, was at least independent. It consisted of ex-army huts left over from the war, and in these I was able to find a couple of rooms and set up an office.

The work on which I now embarked was with adults, men and women who had suffered strokes and who came to me individually for therapy. I found the work fascinating and before long it occurred to me that it might be beneficial to bring my patients together in a little group. For their part, they were fully ready to co-operate in the scheme.

At that time patients were brought by ambulance to one particular hospital called Mayfield Hospital and taken back, also by ambulance, after treatment. At Mayfield I received help from two people in particular: a Nurse Smart and a Mrs. Jenny Somerville, one of the carers at the hospital, who also played the piano. With their assistance, therefore, I embarked on my first attempt at group work for stroke patients. Never having seen it in action or heard of any similar work being carried out elsewhere, I was taking something of a risk. Nevertheless I felt certain in my own mind that it was deeply important to prevent these patients from becoming isolated. Language, I knew, played a vital part in social contacts of every kind. I was hopeful, therefore, that my venture would succeed and, as it turned out, it proved highly fruitful.

If my memory serves me correctly, my first group consisted of eight individuals who had suffered various forms of stroke and were nearly all right-sided hemiplegics. My aim was to create a social atmosphere in which their loss of language would not make them feel isolated. Certainly all of us enjoyed working together and the patients positively loved taking part in these group sessions. One of them, a Mr. Donachy, played the mouth organ and a friend of mine from the College of Education used to bring her percussion instruments. Together we made music and the patients found it all great fun.

About the late sixties or early seventies I responded to an invitation from the Chest, Heart and Stroke Association in London to write an article for their bulletin or journal on my experiences in group therapy. Soon afterwards the same body wrote to me again to tell me that they were hoping to set up a club for stroke patients in Dundee. They asked whether I could recommend a young, enthusiastic person willing to undertake the hard work involved in organising such a club and offering, as I recall, a small fee to the right applicant. Since the projected club was to be run by the Association itself, no NHS ambulance would be available for use by those attending it.

I soon discovered a young woman, a Mrs. Bartlett, who, I was sure, was exactly suitable for the job, being enthusiastic, hard-working, conscientious, and deeply interested in the work. However, amongst other home commitments, she had three children to care for, one not yet at school. I wondered, therefore, whether she would be able to undertake the task. That I myself would be involved in setting up the club was something which I fully recognised and accepted. What I was not prepared to undertake was all the organisation that the work would undoubtedly entail – the writing of letters, for instance, or the making of detailed arrangements. Not without certain misgivings, therefore, I gave the Association Mrs. Bartlett's name and address. I then completely forgot about the matter until I was forcibly reminded of it by receiving a telephone call from Mrs. Bartlett herself.

'Catherine,' she began, 'Did you give my name to the Chest, Heart and Stroke people? Well, I have had a letter from them offering me this post. I have consulted my parents and in-laws and they all agree that I should take it. They will step in to act as baby-sitters or child-minders and do whatever else is necessary in order to enable me to undertake the work.' She accepted the post therefore, and together we set up the club in Dundee. In the recent past she had been a teacher at the Demonstration School and now used her influence to obtain the use of a room there. Here we brought together about a dozen ex-patients from the hospital, all of them stroke sufferers who now found it difficult to communicate. A class was held for them every week.

Since not all the members of the club were outpatients at the hospital, arranging the necessary transport was a considerable undertaking. Nevertheless, Mrs. Bartlett tackled the problems involved with characteristic

determination and enthusiasm and in the end the obstacles were overcome.

Meanwhile I was, of course, working with the group which I had
already initiated. Unlike those attending the new club, the members of the
group had all been outpatients, so that it was not difficult to arrange
ambulances to transport them. Gradually in both groups the numbers grew
and while I worked with one, Mrs Bartlett was proving highly effective
with the other. Our method was to encourage the patients to speak by
playing games involving the use of a few words. We also made music
together and, of course, shared in a cup of tea.

All our work was progressing happily when fate dealt us a fresh blow.
For the second time in my life I suffered a serious car accident, this time
one which left me unable to drive any more. However, I was able to
overcome the difficulty at least in part. It happened that the bus conveying
the nurses to Ashludie Hospital in Dundee passed the end of my road
every morning and afternoon, so I set up a fresh clinic at Ashludie, to
which the out-patients – again, all stroke sufferers – could come. As it
turned out, the new clinic was both successful and enjoyable. By this time
I was doing much research work on the condition of stroke and language
disability and I continued with this until I reached the age of seventy, at
which point I felt it was time to retire. However, my retirement was
destined to be of short duration.

Before long the telephone began to ring. Relatives of four of my former
patients rang to ask what they could do. Since I had left, the patients had
been frustrated and unhappy. Some of them were actually weeping. Could
I go to see them? Though I had ceased work and no longer had a car, I
could manage to reach three of them by bus. A fourth patient was a retired
G.P. in Carnoustie, and in this case his wife was able to take me to him.
Until 1981 therefore, when I left Dundee, I continued to do this work for
four days a week on a purely voluntary basis, spending two whole mornings or two whole afternoons with one or other of the patients. On the fifth
day of every week I would visit Dundee University Library to study
aphasia.

I remember too how important it was to put the business arrangements
on a firm footing from the outset. The first time a patient's relative
telephoned me to ask for my continued assistance I would say: 'Right, I
will come and help you but the first thing we must get straight is my fee. I
do not want to fix it afterwards. If you agree to my conditions I will come
on Monday [or whichever day of the week was suitable in the particular
case]. If you do not agree to my terms the whole thing is off. Right? My

fee will be one cup of coffee each time I come to see your relation. Now if you do not agree, the arrangement is off.' Of course the initial reaction took the form of protests loud and long, but I would insist. 'All right,' I would say, 'if you do not want me, it is off.' In the end the person concerned would agree. As it turned out, the cup of coffee and biscuits which they provided were useful in ways which they would not have expected. Cups and saucers, teaspoons and sugar basins were all props which I used, in the sense that the names of each item constituted familiar words for the patients to practise.

At this stage I must describe the four patients concerned in rather more detail. The first was a Mrs. Baxter. When I first met her I found that she had just decided to give up trying to overcome her difficulties; all she wanted to do was to sit on the corner of the sofa all day and every day. Yet she was a lovely lass – so much so that I used to call her 'Duchess'. Eventually we developed a most happy and rewarding relationship. The same was true of each of the other three patients. Not only did they show unstinting gratitude, they also became highly motivated. I must emphasise at this point how important motivation is in stroke sufferers. I believe that

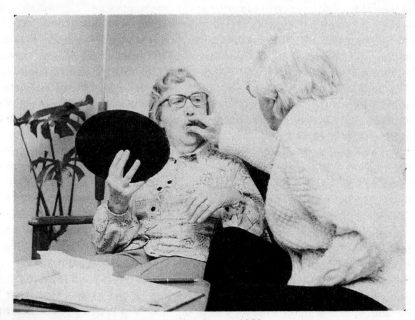

Working with a stroke patient in Aberdeen in 1982.

it is one of the most vital ingredients of all, and would go so far as to say that unless such patients are motivated, it is a waste of time attempting to treat them. In Mrs. Baxter's case I reached a stage at which I could not give her enough to do. She would beat the table with her hands in protest at the fact that I had given her only one page of homework – she wanted more!

The same applied to two other patients, Mr. MacNichol and Mrs. Marshall. All the patients were eager to improve, and did in fact regain a considerable measure of confidence as a result of having someone visiting them twice a week and paying attention to their language.

The fourth patient, as I have already mentioned, had been a GP in Carnoustie. I discovered that he had been an outstandingly good bridge player and very keen. At the time I was living not far from Broughty Ferry and in the light of this information I asked the doctor's wife to bring him along one evening to my house. At the same time I invited two friends named Sonia and Cliff, who were learning to play bridge. They, of course, were delighted and brought with them the manual of instructions which they had been given at the evening classes they were attending. I had arranged with the doctor's wife that I, rather than she, would be his partner. I wanted to control his attempts at communication. Accordingly, I told her to bring her knitting and sit on the other side of the room. When the doctor arrived all this was duly carried out without the slightest fuss or bother, and once he had been introduced to my friends, the four sat down to play bridge. The doctor was a right-handed paraplegic, which rendered him unable to deal cards, though he could collect tricks and put them down. Before we began, therefore, I gave him a large scrubbing brush with specially stiff bristles in which to hold his cards, taking them out and putting them back at will.

All was proceeding smoothly when he noticed the red book of instructions on the table. While the cards were being dealt he picked it up and examined the various diagrams of hands, all made out in the way in which the instructor wanted them played. Then he looked up at my friends in surprise, evidently wondering what sort of people they were to have brought such a book with them. After some further play it came to his turn to declare. 'Doctor,' I said, 'It is you to declare; you have to declare. How many are you going and which suit?' Looking at his hand, he held up two fingers. 'Ah,' I said, 'You are going Two. Two.' At this he repeated the phrase with me, which was exactly what I wanted him to do. 'Two. Two,' he said, so intent upon what he was doing that he was quite unheeding of the other two sitting listening. 'All right,' I said, 'we know how many you are going but we still don't know which suit.' At this he pointed to spades. 'Spades! ' I said, and he repeated it after me. 'Two spades', I reiterated, and again he repeated it. By these means I had persuaded him to use the ability which he had. So thrilled was he at being able to speak the words and understand what he was saying that I really believe he would have gone on repeating them over and over again.

All in all it was a highly successful evening. Long before the doctor took his leave of us that night, he had fully realised that he was the only one at the table who could play bridge properly. My two friends were only learning while I had not played the game since I was about ten, when I had learned the little I knew of it from my grandmother. The outcome was that his self-esteem was greatly increased; he actually felt one up on the rest of us.

Of all human faculties, speech is among the most important. This is a fact that I had always recognised. Yet I believe that it was not until I had had long and close experience of the extreme cases of speech breakdown which I have just described that I realised just how vital a part speech plays in the lives of all of us. In retrospect, I feel, the work I did with the stroke patients was as valuable and rewarding as any I have ever undertaken. I learned so much from it. I discovered that while I could not guarantee to restore my patients to fluency, they could recover the ability to speak and communicate in sufficient measure to enjoy it. Instead of feeling that no one cared about their speech, that they were cast aside, they could learn to live hopefully from one lesson to the next.

Chapter Twelve

Final Thoughts

From 1989 onwards, having been continually in hospitals and nursing homes, I have changed roles. From being the carer, the person who helped others to build bridges, I have become the one who depends upon the care of others. For me it has been a novel experience; being on the receiving end of the caring process is something which I still find difficult to accept. As I write, I am totally dependent on the carers for their willingness, good will and awareness of my particular difficulties and needs; on the nurses and doctors for the pleasant attitude they show towards me while bringing their expertise to bear upon my various disorders; on all of these to treat me not as a mere cypher but as a human being. In this respect some are excellent, others less so.

I believe that the ability to care well for others is greatly heightened if the carer has the imagination to put himself or herself in the patient's shoes and adapt his approach accordingly. When it comes to oiling the wheels of day-to-day living, the capacity to do this is beyond price. Throughout my work with children in speech and drama, this is the attitude I have sought to foster: an imaginative awareness of the person-alities and points of view of those with whom they have to deal, brought out in their behaviour and in the way in which they communicate.

Sixty or seventy years ago, the word used to describe the work that was being carried out in the improvement of speech was 'elocution'; it con-centrated exclusively on how the individual spoke. Today the word is 'communication'. The significance of the change is that nowadays the entire process by which one person conveys meaning to another is taken into account; communication deals not merely with the means, whether verbal or non-verbal, by which messages are imparted and received, but with the actual content of such messages as well. I see communication as a bridge. Any bridge consists essentially of a span with two ends. In communication, one end of the span is the speaker, the other the listener, and both are equally important. Between them extends the span itself which links them, the span called communication. The speaker must speak in such a way that the listener can understand; then he must listen to check that what he has said has been understood. Finally he must listen to the other person's reply.

Any one of us can suffer breaks in our bridge at some point or other but all of us can learn to build bridges that are sound, the sort of bridges that will make us good speakers, good listeners, good thinkers and good companions. I hope that my work has contributed to the building of good bridges in some cases, as well as to the mending of broken ones in others. For all of us, the building of as many bridges as possible is a profitable exercise but two factors are always involved. First the speaker must be clear as well as easy and pleasant to understand; second, the listener must give his attention to what is being said. All of us know of cases in which those speaking to us gabble and gabble, never bothering to speak clearly and having little regard for what is entailed in clarity of speech. Similarly, we are all familiar with the kind of listener who shows little care in listening. Thus it behoves us to do our utmost to develop both ends of the bridge of communication.

Communication is not a subject; it is an integral element in the pattern of personal development in every human being and, as I have tried to explain, it has two halves. The importance of the listening side cannot be emphasised enough. Unless it is positively encouraged it can all too easily be lost sight of. One of the finest ways that I have discovered of helping children to listen (or adults for that matter!) has been the use of the dramatic method as exemplified in plays. So often the amateur actor, whether child or adult, forgets that what is important is far more than the few words at the end of the previous character's speech, though they, of course, are his cue. What he has to listen to and bear in mind is the entire content of what the other person has just said. Once he appreciates this fact and applies it in his everyday life, he is well on the way to acquiring the listening habit. It is the listener's business to listen carefully and work out the meaning of what is being conveyed.

At this point I would cite two examples of breakdown in communication in which I was directly or indirectly involved. They will serve to illustrate two sides of one and the same equation. The first example occurred many years ago in my attic office at 31 King's Street. One late summer afternoon my typist came in to tell me that a man wanted to speak to me. That in itself was not unusual; many parents used to come to see me about their children's speech or because they wanted them to become members of the Children's Theatre. In this case, therefore, I simply asked the typist to bring the man upstairs. Once seated, he began: 'I can see the notice 'Speech Department' outside the door and I wonder if you can help me.' Since he showed no sign of a stammer, I could not at that stage see what form such help might take. Nevertheless I said that I would do all I could to help him. He then went on to explain that he held a responsible position with a building firm, the head office of which was in London. An essential part of his job was to communicate by telephone with head office, giving reports on how the work in Scotland was progressing. 'I have been told,' he continued, 'that they can't understand what I am saying. Unless I improve my speech and make it clearer, some other arrangement will have to be made. I have a home and family, and I can't afford to lose my job.'

I recognised at once that he had a good voice. Certainly he spoke in Doric, the dialect of the area, but he was speaking fairly clearly and naturally to me and it was not costing him any great effort. 'You have a family?' I asked. 'Yes,' he replied, 'two small girls.' (I believe that they were aged between seven and ten). 'How often do you speak what you might call Scottish/English?' was my next question. 'Not at all,' was the reply. He went on to explain that at home or with his friends at work and in the pub he always spoke Doric. I pointed out that when he had to telephone to London he was conscious of the fact that the person at the other end was unfamiliar with the Doric while he himself was equally at sea with Scottish/English. In fact the auditory feedback of speech was inadequate so that he was failing to communicate the messages he needed to convey in a Scottish/English way.

For me this was a fairly tall order and I had to think quickly. 'Well,' I said, 'I will tell you what to do. Go up to Wylie's bookshop and ask for Miss Meldrum. Tell her that I have sent you and that I have asked her to give you a book of good short stories for children of that age – well written stories. When you get it, I want you to read aloud every night to your little girls. You will give them pleasure so that they will follow you, but more than that, you must look at them to make sure that they are following you. Don't go too quickly. In that way you will learn to hear your own voice coming back to you, using the form of language in which the story will have been written, which will be English – written English, certainly, rather than the spoken form, but nevertheless the practice will give you a confidence that derives from hearing your own voice at that other level. Will you do that?'

He thanked me and said that he would. Being an intelligent man, he knew what I was trying to tell him. Then he took his leave. Many weeks passed before I heard from him again and I sometimes wondered whether he had lost his job. Late one afternoon, however, I was having a meeting with my staff in the same little attic office. The room was crowded so that few chairs were available, I remember, that someone had to sit on the floor. A knock came on the door and when I said 'Come in,' it opened and the same man put his head round the corner. As soon as he saw the crowded state of the room he simply said: 'O.K. Thanks very much,' and put his thumb up.

Here then is an example of the use of English/Scottish producing a happy ending. It was not elocution that the man needed, but rather practice in the use of a form of English that would be understood by anyone who spoke the English language. He had crossed the bridge successfully.

My second illustration of the bridge of communication is a more personal one. It exemplifies the assumptions people make about a speaker from the register of the speech he or she uses. I was in Woodend Hospital suffering from a broken leg, so that one of my major troubles was immobility. I was occupying the bed at the end of the ward. Those who have been in hospital will realise that the table for meals, where patients who are mobile take their lunch or supper, is prepared either at the end of the ward or in the middle. So it was at Woodend. In this case the table was at the end of the ward close to my bed. At mealtimes, therefore, all I had to do was to get up and use my zimmer to move to the end of the table. Those other patients who were not confined to bed – there might have been eight or nine of them – would walk across to the table and sit down on the other side.

At my first meal the others began almost immediately to talk, exchange jokes and generally enjoy themselves in a social as well as in a gastronomical sense. Nothing had been said about me, no introductions had been made, nor had any explanation been offered as to why a new patient with a broken leg should be sitting there. The result was that I felt a bit awkward. However, I reflected that for nearly seventy years communication had been my business. 'I don't want to be beaten by this,' I thought to myself, 'but I don't like to begin.' So I simply sat quietly and got on with my meal. Then the same thought recurred: 'No, I'm not going to be beaten.' This time I acted upon it. 'Excuse me,' I said, 'but have you all been here together for a long time?'

They stopped rather suddenly and looked at me. I suppose the question itself had taken them by surprise; it was not about the weather, the food or any similar topic – not, in fact, the sort of question they would have expected from anybody. Then one patient sitting at the end of the table seemed to grasp the situation. 'No, only a week,' she said. 'Oh,' I rejoined, 'I thought you must have known one another for a long time.' I carried on with my meal and so did they. Obviously, however, I had put a spoke in the wheel. Then a patient sitting on the opposite side of the table and diagonally across from me leaned over. 'Ye ken, we thocht you wis ane o' the posh anes, and we didna like to spik to ye,' she said. I laughed. 'Well,' I said, 'you were very far wrong, weren't you?' That was the end of that! Next day I was discharged from the hospital, yet in spite of everything I believe that that episode might have had a happy ending too. They had been suspicious of me on account of my speech. The fact that I spoke a kind of Scottish/English had led to difficulties in communication.

Here, then, are two examples of broken bridges: the one caused by a failure to speak a kind of English that could be understood by everyone, the other caused by the listeners' assumptions about, and prejudices against, that same form of English. Oh, the complexities of communication!

In writing this book it has been no part of my purpose to teach anybody to do anything. Nevertheless, I hope I have shared with my readers the challenges with which I found myself confronted in my work and some of the ways which I discovered to deal with them. One specific aim which was supreme and abiding to me was concerned with children. I wanted them to have the self-confidence that I never had and to be interested in the process of developing themselves. I wanted them to discover the wonder of books and travel, and to have the courage to be original thinkers. I wanted them to have confidence amongst their own contemporaries and in whatever society they might find themselves placed. Arnold Wesker, the playwright, has said: 'The more bridges you know about, the more places you can see.' With that I find myself in wholehearted agreement.

No finer way exists in which to discover yourself than the use of spoken language. Again and again we find that it is the voice that reveals the person. Through the voice we can clearly discern the differences between the arrogant, the rude, the uninterested on the one hand, and those ready to listen to us, share with us, find enjoyment with us in a spirit of happiness and courage on the other. Herein lies the difference between positive and negative personalities.

There is a courtesy in the voice, there is an arrogance in the voice. The development of this faculty and the use of spoken language should be part of a programme of self-development for every one of us. In those who have little or no confidence it can be fostered, nurtured and developed. For this purpose I can think of no better approach than through dramatic work. Clearly the development of such confidence in children depends largely on the attitudes of teachers at school and of parents at home. To succeed in this respect, all teachers must have an awareness of the positive qualities of which I have been speaking. It is vital that all teachers should guard against encouraging in any way the arrogant or the show-off. Here is a trap into which it is all too easy to fall, especially for drama teachers.

This age, with its tremendous emphasis on television, is breeding a far less conversational community than was the case in former times. In consequence, we are in danger of losing sight of the importance of speech. The wiser parents, of course, are aware of the danger and take steps accordingly, but all too many individuals are unfamiliar with the sound of their own voices as used in more formal contexts, for instance when they are addressed by strangers or in strange company. A point that needs to be borne in mind is that everybody speaks differently. Each individual's speech mechanism – the shape of his mouth or tongue, his ability to use his lips or his lungs, is different from that of his fellows and this affects the nature and quality of his speech.

I am a great lover of dialect. To ignore the importance of teaching it would, I feel, be a limiting factor. At the same time, it is also important to encourage children to speak a brand of English that will be understood anywhere where English as such is spoken.

As I look back, I can perceive a pattern that has gradually emerged in my work. Even though I was unaware of it at any given stage, I now recognise it very clearly. The Non-Competitive Festival, The Children's Theatre, Puppetry, the Play and Poetry Competition, The Longacre Players, together with my regular classes in schools – behind all these activities has lain a single overall aim: to enable all the children who came in contact with me in any part of my work to grow in confidence, self-esteem, ability to socialise with their contemporaries and with other people generally, and to understand the value of communication.

Of course I realise the objections that many will put forward. 'Oh, we cannot afford to carry out a programme of work such as you have described. It would be too expensive. We haven't got the money.' To this I would reply: 'Nonsense, I have done it – and I did it on a shoe-string.' In all my time in Aberdeen, at no stage was I accustomed to having ample resources with which to work. I even remember my delighted reaction at being paid a salary for work which I would willingly have done for nothing.

I believe that it took me a year or two after being appointed to discover that such factors as 'estimates' so much as existed, or that I could be applying for financial help each year in order to acquire certain articles which I needed. The reason I was ignorant of these facts was that no one had told me! It was only by accident that I discovered that such possibilities could indeed be explored. One day I was sitting in the corridor of the Town House, waiting to go before the Education Committee to read my annual report. Sitting beside me was Mr. John Dalby, the Superintendent for Music. He made some remark about 'estimates' which forced me to ask: 'What are they?' Only when he had told me did I realise what I had been missing! Nevertheless, even without spending much money, I had been making excellent progress in my field.

Throughout my career I have been accustomed to achieving my aims through a simple and honest approach to my work. It has never involved any major expenditure. My belief that this approach is the right one was reinforced by my experiences in early days in working with the Summer Players. Their real successes were achieved with such artistic economy that to me it was a revelation in itself of how work should be done. I simply adopted the same guiding principle. In all honesty I would say that in financial terms my work has invariably been carried out on a shoestring. The claim that lack of financial support makes such work impossible is absolute nonsense – certainly so far as my field of work is concerned!

We are all aware that in the current climate much talk is being bandied about on the subject of cuts in educational expenditure. Nevertheless, it is my ardent hope that those training to be the teachers of the future in the colleges of education are still being given the opportunity of involving themselves in all the various forms of activity designed to encourage oral expression in its various forms: improvisation, for example, or puppetry, the use of tape-recorders, the production or the writing of plays and poetry and all the other activities which we used in schools and in the Children's Theatre. It is vital for such trainee teachers to understand the potential of such activities for developing their future pupils' self-confidence, self-esteem and courtesy towards others. At the risk of seeming to be making excessive claims, I must assert that what we were aiming at was to build a race of adults fit for future children to live with. Education can and must still afford that.

After all these years I remain convinced that the ability to communicate, to speak, is one of the greatest gifts man possesses. My work as a speech therapist has brought home to me the unhappiness and frustration of the individual who, as the result of a stroke, has lost the power of spoken language and sometimes too the capacity to understand what is being said to him.

It is not only stroke patients, however, who suffer from such breaks in communication. All sorts of people, for all sorts of reasons, may find themselves confronted by the same basic problems. They can destroy the individual's most basic belief in himself and their effects can be quite devastating for the quality of life for himself and for those around him.

Here I find myself, therefore, in my ninetieth year, with my quality of life severely curtailed by blindness, deafness and immobility. Yet I can still look back on past years with pleasure. A large part of my life has been occupied by what is commonly called work, but for me it has been a time of happiness, satisfaction and enjoyment spent with happy groups of people of all ages. Among all my memories, the years I spent with The Children's Theatre and with the stroke patients in Dundee hold a special place. I could not have been luckier.

This, then, is my story. Certainly the influences of my forebears and family, and the traits I inherited from them, have played an important part in my view of life, but so has circumstance. I did not plan a life dedicated to helping children to build good bridges of communication; nor did I plan to rebuild broken bridges with stroke patients. I did not plan anything. It all just happened, and how glad I am that it did!